SO YOU'RE A
KINGDOM
KID

SO YOU'RE A KINGDOM KID

The Blessings and Challenges of Growing Up in the Church

Andrew Joseph Quint

DPI

DISCIPLESHIP
PUBLICATIONS
INTERNATIONAL

www.dpibooks.org

Growing up in the Kingdom has been such a blessing.
God has sent amazing people into my life over and over again.
Most of all my parents Ron and Renée, who have been there
for me in my best times and my worst times.
God is good.

CONTENTS

FOREWORD

Having known Drew Quint and his family for many years through working together in the ministry both in Chicago and Los Angeles, I was curious and intrigued when Drew sent me a copy of a manuscript he had written with the hopes of it someday being published as a book. In this book Drew recounts his life, telling his story of being raised by devoted Christian parents who set standards that reflected the holiness of God.

In this book Drew openly expresses the feelings and doubts he went through at various times in his young life both before and after becoming a Christian. He writes of the times he was inspired by God and all he had to offer, and other times when his heart was filled with turmoil feeling pulled by the world around him. He wanted desperately to be like everyone else and "experience" the life that was not to be available to him.

When I was told the basics of this book before I read it, I was excited. Having raised three of my own children who had experienced much of what Drew wrote about, I thought it could be very helpful for all those growing up in the church. After reading the book it certainly fulfilled all of those expectations, but as it turned out there was much more.

Drew has captured a depth of understanding, honesty and insight in his writing that I found truly captivating. His openness with his own struggles and sin, his battles with pride and deception are both moving and at times humorous but altogether relatable. Additionally his use of the Scriptures and their practical application is rich and draws you to a deeper understanding of God.

What is also wonderful is the picture of true Christian parenting as witnessed through Drew's eyes: tender and loving, devoted to God's holiness with uncompromising convictions, not being influenced by the worldliness around them, trusting in the one who can save souls, seeking to please God and not being swayed by their children's wants and desires. Drew is the example of what such parenting produces.

What I didn't expect in this book, however, was most stunning: its effect on me. I have been a disciple of the Lord for thirty-four years at this writing; twenty-five of those years I have served in the full-time ministry. When I read this book I found my heart being challenged, feeling some of the same struggles in my life that Drew describes in these pages: at times not being as emotionally connected to the fellowship as I should be and not being as tuned in or involved in the spiritual lives of others. I can and have made assumptions about how Christians are doing in their spiritual walk with God, not asking the deep probing questions that reveal where their spiritual heart is. He reminded me of how easy it is to feel comfortable and not be aggressive in my walk with God.

Is this a good book for "Kingdom Kids" to read? Yes! For parents? Yes! Actually, every Christian will both relate to and benefit from this book.

Thank you, Drew.

John Mannel, Elder, Los Angeles International Church of Christ

→ What are the deep probing questions?

HEY YOU!

- Are your parents Christians?
- Has church always been a meaningful part of your family life?
- Were you a biblical scholar by the time you hit the third grade?
- Would life as you know it cease to exist if your parents heard you say a curse word?
- Do you sometimes feel constricted by the rules and regulations from your parents and the Christian lifestyle?
- Do you want a deep and real relationship with God?
- Do you want to go to heaven?
- Do you want to be a Christian?

If you answered yes to some of these questions, this book may be for you. Many young men and women who grow up in Christian households sincerely believe in God and love him, but at the same time, they struggle with feeling restricted by the Christian lifestyle or by their parents' rules.

This was my teenage experience in a nutshell. There were things I wanted to do and try, but I knew I couldn't do them without raising serious concerns at home, and even among people who knew me at church. Freedom was a concept that I had little understanding of because I always felt somewhat trapped.

The reality is that as a young Christian in your teen and college years, you *can* be free, and the possibilities of where God can take you are endless. No dream will be unattainable, no obstacle too great for you to overcome. God wants each of us to fulfill all the potential he put inside of us, and we can only do that when we are living for him, when we are doing things his way.

With God, your life can become something deeper and greater than you can possibly imagine. Even now God is building this foundation in your life.

Through His Eyes

Right now, no matter where you are in your life and walk with Christ, God is calling you; he is asking you to look at your life through his eyes. Growing up in a Christian family has given you an amazing opportunity to know him at a young age, and it is through this opportunity that he will transform your life into an extraordinary journey. I have come to be more thankful for my Kingdom Kid experiences than I can even put into words.

Because I grew up in the church, God has protected me from so much and also entrusted me with so much. Of course, no life is perfect. Kingdom Kids, like anyone else, have plenty of struggles along the way and important lessons to learn, but if we stay close to God, we can remain free throughout all our days to live inspired and inspiring lives.

You have so much to look forward to in living the Christian life: having close friendships with people who know the real you (and still like you!); having fun without guilt and regret; experiencing the joy of the Christian fellowship and all the support and encouragement it provides; the hope of enjoying a pure, godly romance...and if you get married one day, you can be confident that your marriage can last a lifetime because you are committed to building it God's way.

Let's Keep It Real

So get ready! I have a lot of stories to share about how I struggled with my faith and even with my parents during my teen years—they're not all pretty, but I hope they will give you some insight into your own walk with God. At the beginning of each chapter I include a "Keeping It Real" introduction that lets you know about some of my struggles. I hope my story can encourage you to wrestle honestly with your doubts and temptations, and learn to embrace the freedom God offers us all. At the end of each chapter is a chance for you to "Get Real" as you ask yourself some questions and seek honest answers.

I hope this book will help you grow in your love for God and open your eyes to the amazing plans that he has for you.

KEEPING IT REAL
Insecure About Christianity

Ring!

Thank the Lord! The bell for lunch had sounded at Hale Middle School. I was finally able to leave what might have been the most boring math class of all time to go and meet up with my friends. As I made my way to the spot by the cafeteria where we usually hung out, I saw from a distance that Jason was there along with the other guys; usually he wasn't there.

Suddenly I wasn't too interested in walking any closer. Whenever Jason had the opportunity, he loved to find reasons to make fun of Christianity and the way I lived my life. He made fun of a lot of people for a lot of things, but when it came to me he made fun of church.

Looking back, I am not really sure how he was friends with us in the first place, but I knew if I walked over to where Jason was I would get some wisecrack about me living like a Christian and I would be embarrassed in front of everyone. Even if he didn't make fun of me, his mere presence would make me feel insecure about who I was and the Christian fellowship that I was a part of. Math class didn't seem so bad now compared to hanging out with Jason for forty whole minutes!

I stood there for a split second deciding whether or not to walk over there. My options were to eat with Jason and the other guys, search around for a different group, or just stay standing there alone between the classroom building and the cafeteria until another solution presented itself. But the leftover Pizza Hut in my backpack from family time the night before was calling my name, so I decided that pepperonis and stuffed crust were enough to outweigh the possibility of Jason's ridicule. I made my way over to my friends.

"Well how's it going, Drew? Isn't it a hot *&%?! day today?" Jason always cursed extra often around me because he knew I didn't say bad words.

"Yeah, Jason, it sure is," I replied.

"Wouldn't you say that running the mile today in PE would be #@*&% hard, Drew?"

"Yes, it would be darn hard."

"Darn hard? Or $%^*! hard?"

"What's the difference, Jason?"

"Oh, not much difference, just that you are too afraid to curse I guess. Hahahaaaaa!"

"Fine! It's a $%^*! hot day today. There, are you happy? I'm not afraid to curse!"

And so it continued for the rest of a miserable lunch period. You get the picture. I had other experiences like this with other people growing up, but no one else ever made fun of me nearly as much as Jason did. Over the years I tried not to spend too much time around him, but when I was around him and when he made fun of me, it felt horrible. When he humiliated me in front of other people, it felt even worse. → *Depending on the region of the U.S.*

I was always so self-conscious about my church. I always felt like people thought it was weird—or that they would think it was weird if they knew more about it. Experiences like the one I had with Jason in elementary school and middle school played a big role in how I grew up feeling about Christianity. I loved that I got to go to church, and I enjoyed it, but at the same time I was ashamed of it and wanted to distance myself from it. Why couldn't I just be myself? Why couldn't I just be proud of the Christian lifestyle and be cool around my friends as well?

Really? Do kids really make fun of other kids who are doing the right thing?. I don't remember experiencing this. It seems so petty. I can see how real it is in the moment, but this "Jason" seems to be the one w/ issues....

Do they? YES! (the teens)

I have slowly begun to realize that these experiences as a young man played a huge role in my development as a follower of Jesus. In high school I struggled with how my friends viewed me and my Christian walk. I felt like my upbringing as a devout Christian was a reflection of who I was. If people thought Christianity was weird, it meant that I was weird too.

In college I sometimes worried that when my friends visited Bible Talk (our small group Bible study), they would think it was strange and uninteresting. Even today, at the age of twenty-four, I can still struggle with assuming that Christianity is awkward to people who aren't a part of the fellowship.

In school I always stayed far away from people like Jason because they made me feel horrible about myself. The sad part about Jason is that in high school he ended up getting seriously addicted to drugs, and he left our school to go somewhere else. For several years I didn't know what had become of him.

However, a few years after high school I ran into him in a public place, and he was so excited to see me. He told me that he had gotten sober after he left our school and that he was living a much better life. With a grin on my face, I reminded him about how he always used to make fun of me because of my Christian lifestyle. Interestingly, he was the one who was embarrassed this time.

I invited Jason to church that day and sincerely hoped he would come. He never did, but getting the opportunity to invite him allowed me to think back and deal with all of the insecurity that I experienced in my years as a Kingdom Kid. Hearing about what Jason had gone through with his addiction made me realize that the Christian life wasn't something to be ashamed of—it was something to be proud of!

Jason grew up with divorced parents. He struggled to make close friends because of the way he treated people. He probably had deep insecurities that I never knew anything about. I can't help but wonder if things could have turned out differently if I had been different. If only I had been a better friend to Jason growing up, if I had stood proud for Christ, maybe Jason would have been more open to Christianity. Maybe he wouldn't have had to go through some of the things he went though. Who knows? Maybe he would be a disciple today. I know that God has a plan for Jason's life as he does for mine, and I can only pray that God is still working to open his heart.

↓

Hindsight is 20/20 . . .
Ask questions to the teens : i.e.
What will the long term results be
of a bully/deceiver/cheater be? vs.
the long term result of those who
please God?
 - WHAT side do you want
   to be on?

 - How can you help others
   get there?

—

Counting the Cost Questions

• What is high school like when you are a disciple?
   - Pros ⟩ Do they have a realistic perspective?
   - Cons
        - lunch table talk   - skipping school
        - Prom Parties   - boyfriends
        - teachers/authority
          (even if they
           are wrong)

• How will your college decisions be affected by being a disciple?
•   "   "   "   Single life   "   "   "   "   "   "   ?

What Is a Kingdom Kid?

Maybe you haven't heard the term "Kingdom Kid" before. I have been called this by people in my fellowship ever since I can remember. In general, Kingdom Kids are people who have grown up in a Christian home and around a Christian fellowship.

Growing up in a Christian household has its many blessings. For example:

- I grew up with parents who loved God and loved me unconditionally.
- I had close friends who also had parents who loved God.
- My parents never neglected or abused me.
- I grew up with a good conscience.
- I got to go to some pretty cool youth camps.
- My brother and I had a very good friendship, and still do (except for the time he slammed my finger in the front door when I was five).
- Some older guys I admired in the church took the time to hang out with me and teach me about life.
- The list goes on...

Even with all of these blessings, I can still say that growing up in a Christian home isn't a walk in the park. Kingdom Kids experience a unique set of struggles that can be very difficult to overcome at times. But with all the hardship, confusion, blessings and lessons learned, I fully believe there is a very special role in God's plan for everyone who has grown up in a Christian household.

In Deuteronomy 6:5-7, God commands the Israelites,

> "Love the LORD your God with all your heart and with all your soul and with all your strength. These commandments that I give you today are to be upon your hearts. *Impress them on your children.*" (emphasis added)

God commanded the Israelites to take his laws and impress them upon their children so that future generations might live according to his word. God wants everyone to experience the kind of upbringing that Kingdom Kids have had the privilege of experiencing: the opportunity to grow up hearing about him and his truth. God hopes that people will live for Christ, have children, and then teach their children about Jesus and his work in their lives. Once we realize that God wants this for all people, we can begin to understand just how blessed we are to be raised in a Christian environment, even if it comes with its own set of challenges.

The Freedom We Are Fighting For

In one way or another, every Kingdom Kid—every person, really—wants to be free. Being free generally means being unrestricted by outside forces and left alone to do what you please. It is part of our nature as human beings to want freedom. I believe the reason for this is because our Creator made us to be like him. Genesis 1 says that God created men and women in his image. God took all of the beautiful, majestic and eternal things that make him who he is and used them to make us! We have a soul, we have an identity and we have the ability to reason between right and wrong.

Everything in existence has a purpose. Stars burn and provide light, gravity keeps planetary bodies in order, water provides sustenance for plants and animals, plants create oxygen for animals to breathe—everything God made has a set role in the universe. But imagine if an elephant, after noticing a hawk flying through the sky, decided it was time to fly from now on instead of walk. Or imagine if a ballerina decided it was time to play professional football! (Or vice versa?!)

Just as it makes no sense for an animal or person to defy the way God made them, so it makes no sense for us to reject our own purpose by fighting God's will for our lives. The chief purpose of humanity is to have a relationship with our Creator and become more like him; to find our identity in our Father in heaven instead of the empty life offered by Satan. God is certainly alive today and he is free. He wants us to experience freedom as well.

What Do You Really Want?

As humans, we have been given the mental power to desire and choose. Think about your own life. Think about something that you want more than anything else. Something that, if you had it, would make the rest of your problems seem like nothing at all. To give you a few examples, there have been many times in my life when

- I felt that a relationship with a girl would solve all my problems.
- All I wanted was for my friends to think I was great so I didn't have to be insecure.

- I thought I needed to succeed in school, so I didn't have to worry about the consequences of failure.

These desires are not intrinsically bad or sinful. It's not wrong to want a girlfriend; it's not sinful to want friends or to desire success. We absolutely have the freedom to pursue such things, but the problem comes in when they become our god. They can never replace God in our life; they can never give us joy or set us free the way God can.

True Freedom

Consider that you were made to be like God, the One who created everything in existence. Consider where you are going to spend the rest of eternity instead of where you are going to spend the next few years. Wouldn't you say that God is a little more important in the grand scheme of things than a romantic relationship, looking cool around your friends, or getting an A+ on your next chemistry exam?

Although certain laws of nature and spirit may keep us from having anything we want all the time, there is no law that can keep us from becoming everything God created us to be for now and eternity. God's imagination is infinitely greater than ours, and he has envisioned great things for us, but first we have to want his will for ourselves. And once we do, it is amazing how small the rest of our problems become.

This is true freedom: that we may live out the endless possibilities for which we were created and grow closer to our Father in heaven. It is not only a freedom from all of the expectations and pressures of church, but more importantly, it is a freedom from sin that brings us back to God. Jesus is the example. In fact, he is the way!

Your Walk As a Kingdom Kid

Every Kingdom Kid's walk is different. Although we may not all experience the exact same blessings or hardships, we all understand what it means to grow up among a fellowship of believers. Every Kingdom Kid has felt the pressure to <u>live like a disciple when others are watching</u>.

We all know the unhappiness that comes from the guilt we feel when we sin. And we know the anxiety and uncertainty that comes when we aren't sure if we are capable of living the way our parents and fellow church members think we should. Many Kingdom Kids, at one point or another in their lives, have difficulty <u>dealing with all of this pressure and expectation</u>.

The truth is that life for the Kingdom Kid doesn't have to be as difficult as it may sometimes seem. We can feel like we are trapped, but we aren't. We might think our only way to freedom is to leave our relationship with God, but it isn't. The pressure we feel usually has more to do with our own perception than it has to do with reality.

Yes, the pressure from others is real, but it has more to do with what *we* are telling *ourselves* than what others are telling us. It has more to do with what *we* want for our lives and less to do with what *others* want for our lives. I can think of so many times in my life when I felt trapped—like I just couldn't have the things I wanted or I couldn't be the person I wished to be. I would get so frustrated, and at times I acted on my frustration. But every time I tried to break away from my relationship with God, it didn't take long for me to realize that life was empty without him.

There is a road that leads to complete freedom in Christ with our Creator, a road that leads to joy and peace and fulfillment. I know, because God is letting me walk on it. And when I think straight and stop doubting his plans for my life, I am always freer than when I try to live my life without him.

Perhaps this book can help you find your path. Everyone's path is different, but they are all paved by God. As it says in Psalm 119:32, "I run in the path of your commands, for you have set my heart free."

GET REAL

1. Is there a "Jason" in your life—someone who makes fun of your desire to do what is right? What did you learn in this chapter about how to respond to this person?
2. What are some of the blessings that come from being a Kingdom Kid?
3. What are some of the challenges?

KEEPING IT REAL
Thou Shalt Not!

It was day one of my tenth grade school year. I was sitting in my seat in drama class waiting for class to end, and it hadn't even started yet! Then *she* walked into the room...the most beautiful girl I'd ever seen at my school. She sat right next to me, and suddenly I wasn't so anxious about class ending any more. Now I was worried about what in the world I should do!

I thought to myself, *Man, she's pretty. Should I say something? Should I wait for her to say something? I don't know... Oh, it doesn't matter; she doesn't go to church with me, so I can't like her anyway. What's that scripture again? "THOU SHALT NOT DATE A GIRL WHO DOESN'T GO TO CHURCH!"? Yeah, something like that.*

I had given up on the idea of liking her before I even met her. I probably wouldn't even have opened my mouth to say anything if she hadn't spoken first.

"Hey, what's your name?" she asked, in a flawless, angelic voice.

My thoughts were scattered once more. *Name? Who me? Quick, what's your name you idiot!*

"Uh, Drew. My name is Drew," I finally answered.

"Mine's Ashley Smith." (Of course, I'm changing some of the names in my stories, but the people and the stories are real.)

We ended up having a nice conversation that day before the start of class. I learned a lot about Ashley that semester: her religious beliefs, values, dreams and much more. I liked her, and as the semester went on, I was pretty certain that she liked me too. Despite all of this, my conscience never let me pursue her because I knew that if I were to date her I would be compromising my discipleship. She was not what the Bible considers to be a believer, and 2 Corinthians 6:14 says Christians shouldn't be yoked with unbelievers. I was pretty sure dating would count as being "yoked."

I was terrified of what would happen to me if I were to pursue a girl who was not a Christian. So it didn't happen.

Counting the Cost Questions

- How will being a disciple affect your dating relationships?

- How will being a disciple affect your relationships w/ guys?

- What happens if you start liking a non-disciple?

Under Pressure

Kingdom Kids are taught from childhood to fear God and obey his commands, and to honor and obey our parents. Those are good teachings, and I am forever grateful that I grew up in the environment I did, being taught right from wrong. But this fact remains: Like many Kingdom Kids, I felt intense pressure to do the right thing. I worried about disappointing my parents, my church and my friends, and sometimes that worry turned to fear. I felt a lot of pressure—not just from my parents and my church, but from the Bible and from my own conscience as well.

For most of my childhood and on into high school, I felt that there were certain boundaries that I just could not cross. Whether I wanted to or not, whether I was able to or not, I simply couldn't bring myself to break the rules. Something inside just didn't allow me to lie to my parents, cheat on tests, watch R-rated movies, use curse words, go to parties, go out with girls at school, or just be whoever it was I wished I could be in certain situations. (However, you will see that later on in my walk, I did cross many of these lines.)

In Sunday school I was taught over and over again that God didn't like liars, and cheaters would never prosper. My parents used to have conversations with me about why I should only like girls who are Christians. My teen leaders used to express disappointment if I was selfish or reserved when we had teen devotionals.

Understanding the Pressure

Growing up, all children feel some amount of pressure from their parents to act a certain way. In a non-Christian culture, kids are kept from disobedience by the authority of their parents. In a Christian culture, a parent's authority over why a certain action is "wrong" is combined with the divine authority of God. Mom and Dad believe it, the church believes it, and so does God, so there is absolutely no way for you to ever even consider the possibility of proposing the idea of trying to think about breaking the rules!

Throughout most of my life I knew the pressure was there, but I didn't quite understand what it was, where it was coming from, or why it was so powerful in my life. When I was a young boy, the pressure was necessary because my parents were doing their best to raise an obedient child, but as I got older the pressure mounted. As the influences from my friends at school became stronger, the pressure I felt at home and within the church fellowship grew stronger as well.

I was getting old enough to make a decision about becoming a Christian. Well-meaning people at church, trying to make conversation, would ask me if I had begun studying the Bible yet. Every conversation like this amplified the pressure I already felt.

I worried that people at church expected me to act like a disciple even though I hadn't become one yet. My friends in the church were feeling this pressure too, but there was no way for us to talk about it on a real level because we all "knew" and "understood" that the right thing to do was to act like a disciple.

When confronted with a difficult decision, I always fought internally with questions and concerns that my conscience thought it already knew the answers to:

- What will my parents do to me if I don't do the right thing?
- How much will it hurt my parents?
- What will my friends at church think of me?
- What will I think of me?
- What will God think of me?

Responses to the Pressure

Growing up in this atmosphere did amazing things to develop a strong conscience within me, and for that I am eternally grateful. However, the pressure also created a certain level of curiosity that was fueled by my desire for more freedom.

This pressure shaped my early life in powerful ways that I will probably never fully comprehend. When making the decision to get baptized, I had to consider what everyone would think if I decided not to follow Jesus. Every time I started to like a girl who wasn't a Christian I had to first consider, "Is this girl really worth ruining my good name in the church fellowship?" When I spent time with friends at school, I also had to consider, "What will my Christian friends think about me hanging out with these people?"

Once I started recognizing the pressure, I realized how much I hated it. This became dangerous to my spirituality because I started to blame Christianity and my parents for making me feel like I had no choice in how to live my life. It was because of the Bible that I couldn't do what I wanted to do; it was the church's fault that I felt so trapped and guilty. The truth, however, was that I wasn't trapped at all. I *was* free, and all my feelings were exaggerated. I had an unhealthy view of the pressures that surrounded me, and I just couldn't see beyond them.

Healthy Perspective

There are a few very important things we need to come to grips with if we want to gain a healthy perspective on the pressure we feel. First, the pressure isn't going to go away. Second, the negative feelings and effects of it can and do go away. Third, it is possible to live a joyful Christian life of freedom in the midst of this pressure. As Galatians 5:1 says, "It is for freedom that Christ has set us free. Stand firm, then, and do not let yourselves be burdened again by a yoke of slavery."

Whether it's your mom and dad, or leaders in the church, or your Christian friends, or someone else, there will always be people in your life who want you to act a certain way, for better or worse, and *it is a blessing* when people around you encourage you to lead a righteous life. Everyone in our lives is going to pressure us to some degree. The goal is not to break away from this pressure, because the only way to do that would be to eliminate all forms human communication! The goal is to obtain a true sense of self that is influenced by God and by your convictions before it is influenced by any man or organization.

Blessed with a Good Conscience

It is natural to focus on the negative effects that all of this pressure creates in our life, but the truth is that the pressure to be righteous is not all bad! In fact, there is plenty of good that comes out of it. As I said earlier, one of the main blessings that we receive from growing up with Christian parents is a well-developed conscience.

I used to feel different than the other kids at school because I always felt like the "goody two-shoes" of the bunch. I was always afraid to break the rules. I was always out of the loop when kids had fun misbehaving, and I wished my conscience didn't hold me back as much as it did. I felt like I was missing out on a whole lot of fun and adventure because of my good conscience.

But looking back on my life, I realize that a person's conscience can be one of their greatest assets. I was by no means incapable of breaking rules, but throughout my elementary, junior high and high school years, I saw many of my classmates fall time and time again because they couldn't stay out of trouble. And this is only *school* we are talking about, where breaking rules gets you detention or extra homework. In the real world, breaking the rules can get you fired, arrested, fined, jailed or worse! I have already seen many people who just can't keep themselves from stretching the limits of right and wrong, and they have paid dearly for it.

This is why I say that your good conscience as a Kingdom Kid is a greater asset to your future than you know. When I was young, I felt like my conscience limited my ability to live life to the full, but the truth is that it has allowed me to be far more alive and free than other people who are dealing with the consequences of the poor decisions they have made. I have certainly made my own share of dumb decisions, but my conscience was always there reminding me what was right and what was wrong, and for that I am thankful.

GET REAL

1. I shared that "I felt intense pressure to do the right thing. I worried about disappointing my parents, my church and my friends, and sometimes that worry turned to fear." How do you relate to this?

2. In what ways do you feel pressure from your friends at school? Do you often feel torn between pleasing your friends and pleasing your parents and others in the church?

3. I made the point that everyone in our lives is going to pressure us to some degree. Do you believe this is true? Why or why not?

4. When you feel pressure to do wrong, how does your conscience respond?

1.) This is where it is essential that I let the teens decide who they want to be on their own. I only love them, support them, give them advice. But if I push them to be what I want them to be they will feel pressured, manipulated, and insincere. Dear God, please help me inspire your children w/out forcing them. You did not force me and you don't force them.

A.D.
E.W. 2.) The influences & pressures @ school are real. Listen to them.

KEEPING IT REAL
Busted!

I was a junior in high school. At this point I had already been a baptized disciple for more than three years, but there I was…at my friend Sean's house, a beer in my hand, hanging out at a party that a disciple had no business attending. And this wasn't the first party I had been to.

I had enjoyed my Christian life up to that point, but things changed in my junior year. I saw how much fun my friends at school were having (or seemed to be having), and I wanted to be part of it. None of them had such overbearing parents or such a demanding religion to follow, so it seemed like they all did whatever they wanted to do.

When Sean's parents got home earlier than expected that night and busted us all for drinking and partying, Sean barely even got in trouble. If my parents had ever caught me doing some-thing like that, I would have been skinned alive! My friends all dated girls they liked, hung out with whoever they wanted to hang out with, and they seemed free, while I felt like a slave.

I remember going to a teen devotional that year and feeling completely bored. I wasn't having a good time. I wasn't inter-ested in any of the girls at church. I just didn't want to be there. I went to teen devotionals because I felt I had to, but afterwards, I would go out to parties with my friend Russell (who was also a disciple at the time). My parents didn't know what I was doing because I would sleep over at Russell's house on the nights we partied. We would come home super late.

One day when I was sitting in my room at home, my mom came in and asked me what time Russell and I had gotten home after devotional that past Friday.

"Oh, about ten or so I think. I don't really remember," I said. But I remembered exactly what time I had gotten home that past Friday, and it wasn't anywhere near ten. We had gotten back at three in the morning!

"Oh really," my mom said, with a deadly tone in her voice that left me absolutely terrified. "I was talking to Russell's mom the other day, and she said you guys didn't get home till closer to three."

After a short silence and a look in my mom's eyes that nearly stopped my heart from beating, she left my room. I sat there speechless. I really didn't know what to think; I was afraid of what was going to happen next. I knew she wasn't done. Usually something like what had just happened would bring on a thorough interrogation by both parents. (Come to think of it, I am surprised that my parents never invested in a dark room with a spotlight and a lie detector machine...with me, it might have come in handy!)

This issue was far from over and I knew it. A few moments later, Mom came back to say, "Your father and I would like to talk to you. Now."

I already knew what was coming. I considered the possibility of lying my way out of it all, but I had always been horrible at lying. I thought up some ideas anyway.

We went out for a prayer walk.

No, I couldn't say that. It would be utter blasphemy to claim righteousness as an alibi for my late night revelry.

Um, what are you talking about? Russell and I were home; his mom must be mistaken.

Russell's mom wasn't mistaken, and she knew about the other

times that Russell and I had come home late, so shifting the blame onto her wouldn't be wise.

My ideas were garbage. I stopped trying to think of more.

It did not look good. I had no believable alibi, and my parents already had all the facts they needed to prosecute the hopeless defendant who now walked down the hall to certain doom. I entered the living room and sat down across from them, wishing I could find a way to escape the tragic end to my short life here on earth.

Why Freedom Matters

Considering all the pressure that our family, our church friends and our own consciences can put on us, it is easy to see why it can be difficult for Kingdom Kids to comprehend the idea of freedom. Growing up in such a sterilized environment only allows so many options to a Christian kid.

As I mentioned earlier, I grew up often feeling trapped. Most of the time I couldn't even pinpoint the exact reasons I felt this way; I just knew that's how I felt. I looked at my other friends at school and wondered what it must be like not to have this church, this religion and these parents putting pressure on me to be a spiritual person.

I sometimes felt like freedom was a reality beyond my reach. But finding this sense of freedom, the freedom that is foreign to many of us Kingdom Kids, is absolutely essential for our spiritual growth. It is not only possible to find freedom, but it is *necessary* if we are to live as true disciples of Jesus.

God's Definition of Freedom

The apostle Paul told the Corinthians, "Where the Spirit of the Lord is, there is freedom" (2 Corinthians 3:17). I'll say that again: *There is freedom!* This idea is no less true in our day than it was in Paul's day, and it is crucial that we fight to understand what it means for our lives as young Christians. The important thing is understanding God's definition of freedom—the kind that really makes us free...and it's very different from ours.

The first people God made, Adam and Eve, had more freedom than most of us could dream of, yet they still struggled with God's restrictions on their lives. In many ways, Adam and Eve were in a similar situation to the one many Kingdom Kids face. In Genesis 2, we find Adam and Eve living in paradise. They were blessed from the start.

As Kingdom Kids, we must realize how much we have been blessed by the lives that our parents have chosen to lead. Just as Adam and Eve probably couldn't even imagine the barren wasteland of a desert because they had only known God's beautiful garden, so we Kingdom Kids can't even grasp the kind of upbringing that many other kids experience. Compared to the lives of many people around the world, our childhood has indeed been a paradise.

Some children never get to meet their father or mother. Some kids get abused, neglected or sexually molested by their parents or relatives. Many endure the heartache of divorce. Hundreds of thousands of children around the world grow up in horrible family situations and would surely give anything to have parents who care about them, friends who are concerned for their well-being, and a church family that supports and loves them.

I am extremely fortunate to have grown up in a loving household with parents who remained true to their love for each other and true to their love for their children. All this is a gift from God. It is very important to realize all of the good that our parents' discipleship has created in our lives.

Taking Blessings for Granted

But just like the oxygen we breathe, we often take the blessings in our lives for granted because they are all we've ever known. And this is why Adam and Eve are such an instructive example for us. Whether they realized it or not, Adam and Eve lived in paradise. It was the most beautiful existence that any human being has experienced on this earth. Everything was provided for them. They were in direct contact with God and the angels. They lived in a majestic display of natural beauty that would rival any tropical vacation setting we can imagine. To top it off, they both got to spend all of their time with each other, being in love!

In addition to all the beauty, pleasure and joy, there was yet another ingredient to this beautiful paradise which made all the other wonders work together. Genesis 2:16 says, "And the Lord God commanded the man, '*You are free* to eat from any tree in the garden'" (emphasis added).

The freedom to do all they desired is what made the garden a paradise for Adam and Eve. They were free to do anything they wanted in the presence of God (well, almost anything). They had enough freedom to be satisfied for ages.

So all was well and good for Adam and Eve...right? Wrong! There was one kind of fruit on one tree that they could not eat. It was because of this *one limitation* that they did not *feel* free at all! They could not understand God's reason for putting them there. How could God do this to them? They had been chosen by him and were supposedly special to him. He claimed that he "loved" them, but he wouldn't let them eat one simple piece of fruit. This didn't make any sense to them at all! They felt restricted and trapped.

Focusing on What We Can Do

Every Kingdom Kid can relate to Adam and Eve's experience on one level or another. My parents didn't let me watch *The Simpsons* because they felt Bart was a bad influence. And that wasn't all. Our entire family used to act awkward if actors on TV kissed for longer than three milliseconds. I couldn't play certain video games. I couldn't watch certain movies. I couldn't hang out with certain kids at school. There were a number of things that I was not allowed to do, and these rules frustrated me. I did not feel free.

But remember this: The piece of fruit that Adam and Eve were drooling over ended up destroying their paradise. We Kingdom Kids all know the story because, like David and Goliath, Sampson and Delilah, Joseph and his brothers, it was read to us at bedtime and in Sunday school over and over again when we were young. We know that despite the warnings of their loving Father, Adam and Eve still listened to the serpent, the father of all lies and evil. They ate the fruit and brought God's discipline raining down upon their once-happy lives.

Adam and Eve had not always felt such temptation to venture beyond the boundaries God had set. They very much enjoyed Eden and had no reason not to. Anything beyond what they knew in paradise probably scared them. As a young boy I was so taken by my parents' influence that I was practically terrified by anything that wasn't allowed. If kids at school said bad words, I got uncomfortable and embarrassed. If anything even remotely impure came on television, I immediately turned the channel. I was conditioned to desire a more righteous way of living.

As I got older, I became more and more bothered by all the restrictions I had to comply with. As I became a teenager, all of the things my parents said *no* to, I wanted to *know* more about, but I did not feel at all free to pursue this knowledge. As it says in 1 Corinthians 10:23, "'Everything is permissible'—but not everything is beneficial. 'Everything is permissible'—but not everything is constructive."

Freedom to Choose

Now, there is a key part of the story of Adam and Eve that Kingdom Kids must understand, even if it scares their parents half to death. *Adam and Eve were actually free to eat the forbidden fruit.* We know this because they ate it! Sometimes when we read the story, we picture an electric fence around the tree, as if God were blocking off part of the garden from Adam and Eve. But that's not how it was. And the same is true today.

As humans, we have the freedom to be like our Father in heaven. We can devote ourselves to a relationship with God, which will last forever, or we can devote ourselves to the animalistic desires of the flesh, which will last only a short while. This all has been left up to us. Even if we feel pressure to do the right thing, no one is ever going to force us to study the Bible, to make a decision to follow Jesus, or to be baptized. We have the freedom to choose.

God allowed Adam and Eve to eat the fruit, but there were consequences. In the same way, as Christians, we have the freedom to do anything we wish. With this freedom comes the enormous responsibility of dealing with the consequences of the actions that we take, and this is an essential aspect of our relationship with God.

Why is this freedom so important? Because without it, you cannot be YOU. If people didn't feel free either *to* follow God or *not to* follow him, we wouldn't be capable of having a sincere love for him. "Our voluntary service He requires, not our necessitated," wrote John Milton in *Paradise Lost* (Book 5, lines 529–530). And this is what makes us so different from every other being that God has ever created. Our freedom is absolutely necessary in order for us to develop a close relationship with our Creator—to enjoy his friendship that will last an eternity and his fatherhood that will never fail.

Without our freedom we would not be able to be like God, because he himself is free. God can do whatever he wants, and he loved us enough to grant us the same amazing gift. We are not robots programmed to obey our master in everything. We get to choose whether or not to follow his ways and accept his love.

During childhood we get freedom in small doses because we are immature, but we get more freedom as we grow older. Once we decide to become followers of Christ, we all must grasp, both intellectually and emotionally, that we have the complete freedom to decide to follow God, or Satan, or ourselves, or Justin Timberlake, or LeBron James, or whoever else we choose. We need to be confident that we have this freedom. The choice must be ours, and it is.

GET REAL

1. In what way is God's definition of freedom sometimes different from yours?
2. What are some blessings God has given you as one who is growing up in the church?
3. In what ways have you, like Adam and Eve, not been grateful for these blessings?
4. Even though in your church fellowship you might feel some pressure to become a Christian, is it clear to you

that you do have the freedom to choose? Put into your own words what it means that you have freedom to choose whether to become a Christian or not.

Teach the teens the consequence of their actions. Don't tell them what to do. Ask them what will happen if they choose option A or option B or vice versa. Can they accept the consequences.

KEEPING IT REAL
Misery

I sat there on the couch across from my parents dreading the upcoming conversation. I knew there was no way out. My parents always had these strange powers over me. All they had to do was look me in the eye, and I could not say anything but the absolute truth, no matter what they were asking me, no matter how much the truth might seal my doom.

"So, Drew, do you want to explain this whole mix-up about you and Russell returning late at night?" my father asked.

I had no recourse. I knew that once one truth came out, the floodgates would be thrown open.

"I didn't get home at ten the other night. We got home much later than that," I muttered under my breath, just loud enough to be heard.

"What were you doing?" my parents asked in unison.

"Just went to a party at a friend's house."

"Whose house?"

"Our friend Sean."

"Was there alcohol?"

"Yeah."

"Drugs?"

"Yeah."

"Did you have any of it?"

"Alcohol yes, but no drugs."

"Who drove you home after the party if you were drinking?"

"Uh, um...I did."

My parents couldn't believe what they were hearing.

This, coming from their son who was a "disciple"?! I had lied to my parents, I went to a party, I drank alcohol, and then I drove. Now the truth was out. I sat there awaiting a response. I got a heart-wrenching stare of disappointment and then silence that made me feel guiltier than I had felt since I accidentally said the "S-word" when I was seven years old.

"What were you thinking?" was the first of innumerable, unanswerable questions that came from my parents.

I sat and listened until they finished. While I sat there in silence, searching for an explanation for my embarrassing actions and misconduct, I began to ask myself some questions of my own.

Why? Why was I going to parties? Why was I bored at church? Why was I not acting the way I knew God expected me to act? And then something occurred to me that I hadn't been able to verbalize or even conceptualize up until that very moment.

I was unhappy with Christianity. I had never actually said it to myself until just then. I was unhappy with going to church, and I wanted to be happy, so I was searching for happiness elsewhere. But then something else occurred to me: I wasn't happy at these parties either. I actually spent most of my time feeling guilty at the parties. And then it hit me like a ton of bricks: I couldn't be happy being a Christian and I couldn't be happy not being a Christian. I couldn't be happy at all.

I sat there across from my parents, and for the first time in years, I burst into tears, thoroughly distraught over the miserable reality of my life.

Q: (to teen disciples) ... Are you happy in your relationship w/ God?

Chasing Happiness

As we learned in the last chapter, the scary thing about freedom is that it is so often misinterpreted and misunderstood. There are many avenues toward "freedom," or what people *think* freedom is for them, but often these roads actually lead further away from real freedom. Most people associate freedom with happiness, and this connection is a natural one. We usually feel happy when we get what we want. If we have freedom, then we are free to chase after desires that we think will make us happy.

But chasing happiness can be extremely dangerous in certain circumstances. Drugs, sex and alcohol might make us feel happy, but only for a short time. Academic and career success might make us feel happy, but what happens when we fall short of the goals we have set for ourselves? Let's come to a clearer understanding of the type of happiness that we should be searching for.

Chasing the Wind

A famous writer, H.L. Mencken, once described Puritanism—a

version of Christianity practiced by early American colonists—as "the haunting fear that someone, somewhere, may be happy."[1] Though this sentiment would obviously be an exaggerated and false description of Christianity, there were times when I felt this way growing up. Sometimes my feelings were so strong that I wanted to break away and rebel just to prove to myself that I could do what I wanted to do.

Many Kingdom Kids experience similar feelings. After growing up in a Christian fellowship their entire lives, they decide that they no longer want to be tied down by the regulations of the Bible, and they become rebellious (often far more rebellious than necessary!) in order to feel like they are free to find happiness. But there is a monumental difference between *feeling* free and actually *being* free.

Count the Cost of Saying No to God

If the pressure to live up to godly expectations and the frustration of feeling trapped become too much for you to handle, you can certainly run away from home and stop going to church. For a short time, you might feel great about not being surrounded by people who pressure you to live a certain way. You might feel much happier than you did before.

However, you will have just left an entire community of people, most notably your parents, who love you more than anyone will love you in the world. And I don't care who you are, *everyone* desires to be loved and cared for; everyone desires to feel part of a family.

You can go do drugs right now—weed, cocaine, heroin, pick your poison—and for a few hours you might feel happy and satisfied with life...but unfortunately, once you are sober again, you will realize that your grasping for freedom and happiness

---

1. Bruce L. Shelley, *Church History in Plain Language,* Updated 2nd Edition (Dallas, TX: Word Publishing, 1995), 292.

has led you to a greater captivity than you had in the first place. In fact, you may even find yourself heading toward addiction, which is one of the greatest human captivities of all. And it certainly does not bring happiness.

You can go date a wonderful, super good-looking boyfriend or girlfriend, and for a time you may feel ridiculously happy. But unfortunately, if there is not a real foundation to support your relationship, over time your "love" will be easily swept away. Maybe another guy will sweep her off her feet, or maybe a better-looking girl will grab his attention. The insecurity and heartache that will accompany all of this will feel like anything but happiness. We don't realize that the "freedoms" we fight so desperately to have can end up owning us instead.

The examples I gave may sound extreme to you, or maybe not. Either way, they help illustrate the point that the things we think will bring us happiness can end up being nothing more than a recipe for a life of even more restriction than we had before. The reason all of these desires and "freedoms" fail is because they are based on things that don't last. They are fueled by our sinful nature.

All Your Wishes Are Granted?

A friend of mine recently asked me what I thought my life would be like now if God had given me all the things that I wanted so much when I was in high school and college.

- What if I had all the popularity?
- What if every girl that I liked could have been mine?
- What if I could have gone anywhere I wanted and done anything that made me feel happy?

I thought about it for a few seconds and realized that if God had been a genie and had granted me all my wishes, my life would be an absolute mess. One girl that I liked ended up having two kids before finishing high school. Another girl that I liked got really into drugs. A lot of my party friends from high school are still living party lives as if they were teenagers...and they are in their mid-twenties.

I could honestly write another book about all the ways my life would be so much more difficult if God had given me all the things that I thought would bring me happiness as a teenager.

Maybe you're not tempted by things like popularity, dating relationships and drugs; maybe you just want to escape all the pressure by running away from it. But I'm sorry to tell you: That plan won't work either. Our problems will never go away unless we deal with them directly.

The following scripture in Jeremiah speaks perfectly to what we are talking about:

> "Therefore, this is what the LORD says: You have not obeyed me; you have not proclaimed freedom for your fellow countrymen. So I now proclaim 'freedom' for you, declares the LORD—'freedom' to fall by the sword, plague and famine. I will make you abhorrent to all the kingdoms of the earth." (Jeremiah 34:17)

→ God gives us the things we ask for even if they aren't good for us.

I can easily imagine Jeremiah speaking these words to the Israelites with an almost sarcastic tone. Jeremiah was known as the weeping prophet because his entire life he spoke the message of God to Israel, and they never received his words with open hearts. So God decided to give them the "freedom" and "happiness" that they were aiming for.

Shame on us if God ever has to take this approach to deal with our stubbornness! He will if he has to, but surely he doesn't want to.

The Frustration of Running and Chasing

The fact is, as long as we are running away from something, or desperately chasing after things that will not last, we are in no way free or truly happy. When I was running after "freedom" by going to parties, I was risking my freedom by driving under the influence! I was risking trading a life under my *parents'* authority for life under the *governmental* authorities in court!

Matters become even worse when we are running away from one thing and desperately chasing something else at the same time. Sadly, many Kingdom Kids find themselves in this exact predicament. They decide to give up the Christian life in pursuit of something worldly that they think will be more fulfilling, but they end up just running, never at rest—they're exhausted from chasing happiness in the world *and* running away from the grasp of Christianity.

And believe me, I have been there. I tried it myself for a while. I felt like the pressure of the church was too great a burden, and I tried to convince myself that the world offered me a peace and joy I could never find with God, even though I knew those worldly things could never last.

There are things in the world that appeal to us and seem to be exactly what we are missing in life, even if we know in our minds that these things won't last forever. And to make matters seem even more insurmountable, it sometimes feels like the pressure we feel from other Christians will last forever. But remember Satan's lies to Adam and Eve in the garden, convincing them that God was holding out on them.

Stop fighting God and start fighting the right battle. We all need to fight for true freedom that will last an eternity: the freedom to stop running and stop chasing; freedom from the pressure of other people; and freedom from our own sinful nature. This is the freedom that brings true happiness.

Grace for the Kingdom Kid: Real Freedom

We *can* find this freedom as Kingdom Kids. In fact, it's been right under our noses our entire lives! His name is Jesus, his solution is grace, and our freedom is found in a relationship with our Creator.

I believe with my whole heart that God wants his children to be happy, and I also believe that he wants us to be free from the slavery of sin.

In the story of the Bible (and as a Kingdom Kid I would assume that you have some knowledge of what goes on between Genesis and Revelation), we see that when God's word was first presented to the Israelites, it caused a lot of issues. The law was nearly impossible to live up to, so the Israelites had to sacrifice animals and perform countless rituals just to protect their salvation. Fortunately, God's plan was always that his Son Jesus would descend from heaven and free humanity from the impossible expectations of the Law.

Interestingly, it seems that many Kingdom Kids go through this same kind of experience in their own lives. We grow up being taught the expectations of the New and Old Testaments. We also learn the expectations of our parents, teen leaders and fellow church members. Although their expectations are certainly well-intentioned and rooted in their love for us, these expectations can become almost impossible to live up to.

Surely our parents and fellow Christians continue to love us, regardless of whether we meet their every expectation or not, just as God continued to love the Israelites even when they disappointed him. But nevertheless, at some point we will eventually fail in one way or another, just as the Israelites failed to live up to the expectations of the Law that God had set before them.

When I began to rebel against my relationship with God, I did not gain (or understand) real freedom at all. I was chasing happiness wherever I thought I could find it, and as I said earlier, I came to realize that I could not be happy in the church, but I could not be happy in the world either. I was searching for fulfillment in the world while the truth of God's word remained imprinted upon my heart, leaving me drowning in guilt all of the time. I couldn't even enjoy my life of sin! I didn't know what to do, and I felt hopeless. Thankfully, there is a man in the Bible who experienced a similar struggle: the apostle Paul. He wrote:

> We know that the law is spiritual; but I am unspiritual, sold as a slave to sin. I do not understand what I do. For what I want to do I do not do, but what I hate I do. And if I do what I do not want to do, I agree that the law is good. As it is, it is no longer I myself who do it, but it is sin living in me. I know that nothing good lives in me, that is, in my sinful nature. For I have the desire to do what is good, but I cannot carry it out. For what I do is not the good I want to do; no, the evil I do not want to do—this I keep on doing. Now if I do what I do not want to do, it is no longer I who do it, but it is sin living in me that does it.
>
> So I find this law at work: When I want to do good, evil is right there with me. For in my inner being I delight in God's law; but I see another law at work in the members of my body, waging war against the law of my mind and making me a prisoner of the law of sin at work within my members. What a wretched man I am! Who will rescue me from this body of death? Thanks be to God—through Jesus Christ our Lord! (Romans 7:14–25)

The inner turmoil that Kingdom Kids face was also experienced by disciples in the first century. Paul was unable to make sense of the battle within his heart between good and evil without the guidance and rescue of Jesus. As Kingdom Kids, our path to freedom begins and ends with Jesus. Jesus came to this earth that all might be saved from the slavery of sin. Kingdom Kids live under the "Law" of the Bible and Christianity's expectations their entire lives, and this Law is good because it shows us the will of God; but to be set free we must find a true relationship with God through Jesus.

Our inability to find freedom comes from trying to attain it by either running away or chasing things that won't last. The freedom that God wants for us will lead us to a place where we neither have to run from anything nor chase anything, but we can simply *be* who we already are! And who are we? We are God's most beautiful creation: mankind. We were created in his image to have a relationship with him; to be his children, his friends, his servants, and much more. This is the reason for grace in the life of the Kingdom Kid: that we may finally be able to be what God created us to be—not because others want us to, but because *we* want to.

We don't have to create our own freedom, because it has already been created for us! We have only to take hold of it by opening up God's word and allowing him to work in our lives. Ephesians 3:12 says, "In him and through faith in him we may approach God with freedom and confidence."

Growing up surrounded by devout Christians, it is easy for Kingdom Kids to forget what the ultimate goal is for their lives. When church becomes about living up to expectations and pressures instead of about having a relationship with God, we lose touch with what Christianity is really all about, and we are not free.

Many important things in our lives are decided by the people we spend our time with: our friends, relatives, love interests and so on. We can't live without them (even though sometimes it feels like we can't live with them either!). Human beings were created to have relationships. If you aren't sure about this, just ask anyone if they enjoy feeling lonely. And real happiness is found in a relationship with the One who will never fail us and never leave us.

We as humans have been given a choice to either live for ourselves or for something greater than ourselves. If simple happiness is my first desire, then I live for myself. If true freedom is my first desire, then I live for God. I recognize that the journey of a relationship with God is my purpose, and *real* happiness is a byproduct of that purpose put into action.

As Paul says in Romans 8:1–4:

> Therefore, there is now no condemnation for those who are in Christ Jesus, because through Christ Jesus the law of the Spirit of life set me free from the law of sin and death. For what the law was powerless to do in that it was weakened by the sinful nature, God did by sending his own Son in the likeness of sinful man to be a sin offering. And so he condemned sin in sinful man, in order that the righteous requirements of the law might be fully met in us, who do not live according to the sinful nature but according to the Spirit.

You Aren't Trapped

When we are members of a church, to some degree we will always have people telling us how to live, what to do and what not to do, who to date and not date, who to hang out with and not hang out with, what movies to watch and not watch. We hear sermons; people give us advice. As I have already said, it is easy to begin to feel trapped in all of this, especially if we disagree with it.

One time when I was very young, I jumped into a pool. Just before I hit the water, I realized how dumb I was...because I didn't know how to swim yet! I came up out of the water terrified, flailing my arms around for what felt like ages, trying to keep my head above water. I was beginning to sink when it occurred to me, *Why don't I just stand straight up? I am in the shallow end!* I had fooled myself into thinking I was in danger, when in reality I was fine. I felt trapped by the water around me, powerless to escape. But I wasn't trapped at all! All I had to do was get over my fear and think rationally.

It can be the same way with our walk with God. When I didn't agree with what people told me I should do, I felt trapped and didn't know how to handle it. I didn't realize that I could just stand up! I could stand up and read my Bible for myself, searching for answers. I could stand up and ask questions if I didn't understand. I could stand up and be honest if someone hurt my feelings. I could stand up and have a mature conversation, discussing things I didn't understand, and being willing to hear what others had to say. All I had to do was get my head out of the frustrations and feelings of having no way out, and focus on the fact that God was still there, willing me to live a free life with him.

Furthermore, I didn't realize how fun it would be once I learned to "swim"! Once I learned how to live in the fellowship without being troubled by the pressures (some of them were real, some were just in my own head), it became so much more fulfilling to humbly give myself to serve God and his church.

For me, standing up in the shallow end meant realizing that everyone had opinions about how people should live as disciples. However, the only opinion that mattered was *God's*, which isn't really an opinion, it's the truth! God's word clearly states that he blesses humility (James 4:6). No, I didn't say, "God blesses blind obedience to other Christians who tell you to do things"; I said, "God blesses humility." Humility helps you realize that other people in your church might just have some advice that can save you. Humility tells you that God can use people in the fellowship to help you, and it reminds you that you need that help.

Fair Play

Now think about this: Many of the expectations that other people in the fellowship can have for us—things like expecting us to go to church and read our Bible and refrain from worldly dating relationships—are similar to the expectations that *we* have for other people in our church! Sometimes we expect everyone around us to leave us alone and not judge, even while we ourselves are judging them. (Remember the verse about taking the plank out of your own eye?!)

If we are going to call foul every time we feel trapped by the church, then the church should be allowed to call foul every time we expect it to be perfect! Since the church is made of people, it will never be perfect.

Your Choice

God hates sin; he says so in the Bible. Instead of being frustrated with people who call us to live the life that God asks us to live, we should be grateful that there are people in our lives who preach the Word. Now, it would be one thing if we were forced to live like disciples, but we aren't. You are free to stand up in the shallow end, or drown in it, or not even jump in the pool of discipleship at all. I can attest to the fact that standing is far better than drowning, and swimming is far better than lying on the pool deck getting water splashed in your face.

This freedom is a crucial element of our spiritual lives. Though we do not always feel free, we *are* free, by the will of God. As we saw with Adam and Eve in the last chapter, we too are free to choose the life we want to live; it is *our* choice and ours alone.

Once I realized these things, an enormous weight was taken off my back. Though at times I still felt (and feel) the pressure to live in a godly manner, I have learned how to deal with it and keep a firm grip on my relationship with God, which always makes me feel the freedom and the true happiness that I so deeply desire.

GET REAL

1. Why can chasing after happiness lead to an empty life?
2. Do you see some ways that you are chasing after happiness rather than just seeking to be obedient to God? If so, what are they?
3. If all your wishes for happiness were to come true, how might it not be best for you?
4. Write down how you do or do not relate to the following statement about some teens who grow up in the church: "They're exhausted from chasing happiness in the world *and* running away from the grasp of Christianity."

KEEPING IT REAL
Oblivious

This is a conversation I had my freshman year in college with my best friend, Andres. We were sitting around at his house trying to study for school, but mostly doing nothing academically productive.

"Hey Drew, are you interested in anybody these days?" asked Andres.

"Naw, man, there isn't anyone."

"Are you sure? Because you really seem to enjoy talking to Maria a lot."

"Haha! Now that's funny. No, man, we're just friends. I'm not interested in her at all."

"Lies." Andres grinned and pointed a finger at me.

"Do not accuse me of lying! You hate it when I do that to you!"

Andres threw his hands in the air. "Is it really possible for someone to be this oblivious? Okay fine, Drew, you're right, I don't think you're lying to me. But you are lying to yourself. I'm telling you right now that you like Maria."

"Sure, Andres. You have no idea what you're talking about."

Well, to make a long story short...later on that year, I started to realize that I did in fact like Maria.

Be Honest with Yourself

We were created to be free and love God, but this may not always be where our hearts are. And sometimes it can be difficult to figure out and then admit what's really going on inside. As you can see from the conversation I had with my friend Andres, I am not always good at being honest with myself. I had the same problem in high school when it came to how I was doing spiritually.

The interesting thing about my spiritual walk up to the point when my parents caught me partying is that even though I got into trouble and didn't feel happy with Christianity for a while, I never doubted that Jesus was the way, nor did I doubt that I needed a relationship with God. I had grown up being taught the truth of the Word, and I had never come across any argument effective enough to make me not believe. I understood the gospel and believed it in my mind, but my heart had trouble connecting.

I'm not the only one who has trouble knowing the truth about myself. Disciples in Galatia apparently had the same problem:

> You, my brothers, were called to be free. But do not use your freedom to indulge the sinful nature; rather, serve one another in love. The entire law is summed up in a single command: "Love your neighbor as yourself." If you keep on biting and devouring each other, watch out or you will be destroyed by each other. (Galatians 5:13–15)

As you can see from this scripture, Paul felt like he needed to remind the Galatians that they were indeed free. Paul is basically saying, "You guys are free. Did you hear what I just said? YOU GUYS ARE FREE! So you better act like it or else you are going to ruin it for each other!" They did not realize that they had been set free to love God and other people.

Although we may comprehend God's purpose on a mental level, it is so much more powerful to feel it in the heart, and in order to grasp God's purpose with our hearts, we have to genuinely desire it. We must believe the Bible when it tells us we should want God's will for our lives; we should believe people when they tell us we should want it, *and we should believe ourselves when we tell ourselves we should want it.* And since God is indeed alive, it is so powerful if, out of *free* will, we choose to do *his* will. But how do we get to this point?

It is important to realize that God designed us to seek him. And he didn't design us to fail! No matter how difficult the task may seem, the fact is that our hearts are fully capable of desiring God because this is what we were designed to do when God created us.

First Step

The first step is to be completely honest with where you are right now in your life. You can't move forward without first assessing where you are now. What do people look like if they don't look in the mirror every once in a while? Or what would happen if you took a road trip without first checking to see how much gas you have in the tank? Before we continue on our spiritual road trip, we must check how much gas is in the spiritual tank. You may be thinking to yourself, "How do I do that?" My first answer is that everyone is different and you need to look through the Bible yourself and seek advice from the spiritual people that God has put in your life to help you. My second answer is that to know where you are often requires you to know what you actually want.

What do you want?

What Do You Really Want?

A large part of who we are is revealed by our desires. Most of our actions are dictated by our desires. What we eat, what we wear, who we spend our time with, whether we are happy, whether we are sad...so many areas of our life are affected by our desires because they are such a big part of who we are.

So I will ask the question: What do you want? Notice that my question wasn't, "What does God want for your life?" and my question wasn't, "What do your parents want for your life?" The question was: "What do *you* want? What do *you* desire for *your* life? What do *you* desire for your future? What do *you* want right now?

If I were to go around asking that question of people, more times than not I would get the response, "Um, I don't know what I want." Sometimes people are being honest, and they really don't know what they want; but many times, people are too embarrassed to be honest with themselves (and other people) about what they really want.

Our desires are with us all the time, and they play an important role in who we are as people; we shouldn't be embarrassed about them. Our thoughts gravitate to the things we desire. We spend a lot of our time thinking about the things we want,

What do I day dream about?

When we daydream, we think about the type of person we want to be, the places we want to go, the people we want to be around. Our thoughts are special and sacred. They provide valuable insight into who we are as people.

Be Honest

So I ask you now to consider this: What have you been thinking about the most today? What have you thought about most in the past week? What have you thought about the most in the past month or year? If you can be honest with yourself in answering these questions, you will have a much clearer insight into what you want.

Now maybe what you really want right now is not a relationship with God. It's okay to admit that! Pretending you want a relationship with God won't change the facts! The good news is, we can grow and our desires can change.

When I first asked myself this question back when I was a junior in high school, I came to the conclusion that what I wanted most wasn't God or Christianity; I actually just wanted to be happy. This desire was the basis for most of my actions. I was willing to lie to my parents and do things that I really didn't feel comfortable doing because I was trying to find a way to be happy. I wanted the girl I liked at the time to like me back. I wanted to be popular. I wanted people to think that I was awesome. I thought these things would make me happy. I thought about them more than anything, far more than I thought about all the righteous things I wanted to accomplish for God.

Being completely honest about my deepest desires and what I thought about most was very sobering, especially when I knew in my heart that most of my desires weren't going to last. When I compared the empty happiness I was pursuing with the fullness of the promises of God, it was obvious to me what the better choice was, but my heart just didn't want to recognize it.

I wanted a lot of things that weren't going to last, and I had good reason to want them; in some ways, they would have made me happier temporarily, in that moment. But when I came to the conclusion that none of my worldly desires would get me to heaven and none of them would last forever, I realized I had to work to get my heart to where it needed to be.

We Can Rebuild

As I have said, before we can live a free and effective spiritual walk, we must be honest with ourselves about where we are right now. Once I was able to pinpoint the exact thoughts and desires that were keeping me from growing in my relationship with God, I was able to begin rebuilding my life spiritually. Granted, I could have decided not to pursue a relationship with God. I could have just as easily closed the book on my spiritual journey and fallen away, but I knew that this strategy led nowhere.

The Bible says, "The fear of the Lord is the beginning of wisdom" (Psalm 111:10), and I knew enough to fear a life without God—the emptiness, the shallowness, the temporary nature of all that the world has to offer. This was a good starting point! And once I realized this truth, I was ready and able to develop a sincere love for God and his purpose in my life.

John 8:31–32 says, "If you hold to my teaching, then you are really my disciples. Then you will know the truth, and the truth will set you free." This same principle can be applied to the level of honesty we hold within ourselves. If you are honest with yourself about who you truly are and what you really want, you will be set free because you will be able to begin seeking and holding to God's purpose for your life.

Desire Something Greater

You may be thinking to yourself, "Well, that's great that I now understand where I am...BUT I STILL CAN'T HELP THAT I WANT ALL THESE THINGS THAT ARE NOT FROM GOD!" It is completely understandable if you are thinking this. Believe me, I have felt that way! The fact is, the sinful nature continues to wage war against the spirit; and that battle will continue as long as we live on this earth. It is very difficult to escape our sinful desires. It is ultimately the working of the Holy Spirit that allows us to repent and live under the grace of God. But even though it's difficult, God still demands that his disciples live in step with the Spirit as we follow Jesus:

> Finally, brothers, whatever is true, whatever is noble, whatever is right, whatever is pure, whatever is lovely, whatever is admirable—if anything is excellent or praiseworthy—think about such things. Whatever you have learned or received or heard from me, or seen in me—put it into practice. And the God of peace will be with you. (Philippians 4:8–9)

Why did Paul want the Philippians to think about all of these things? Probably because they are better than the worldly alternatives. Why think about worldly things when there are so many godly ones to focus on? Why believe in something fake when you can believe in something real? Why do something the wrong way when you can do it the right way? Why look at something ugly when you can look at something lovely?

The only way you will ever be able to be free of your worldly desires is to find something you believe to be *better*. Righteousness is better than sin; but if you don't view it as better, you won't want it. Until you believe in your heart that a relationship with God is better than a relationship with the world, you will not be able to get over your worldly desires.

Let's Go for Something Better

This principle works in other areas as well. When I was in high school, there was a girl at church who I really liked, but unfortunately, she did not feel the same way about me. I never actually got over her until I met another girl who I thought was even more interesting and beautiful than she was, and I was finally released from her spell.

In middle school, I used to watch TV and play video games all the time. You can imagine what a productive person this made me! I had trouble focusing on my homework; I didn't want to spend time with God, and my mom was always hounding me about cleaning my nuclear disaster of a bedroom. I was well on my way to becoming a lifelong couch potato. But one day, I picked up a few books—business books, spiritual books, some good novels—and I started to read. (I know, it's shocking, right?!)

Those books were amazing. They grabbed my attention in a way no video game ever had. I ended up becoming a business major because of the business books (which eventually led to me moving to Cambodia, where I now live, working with nonprofits). I ended up getting into writing because of the spiritual books (which led to this book being written!). The point: My life changed when I realized that I liked reading books more than I liked watching TV or playing video games.

Now, let's take that principle and apply it again to our relationship with God. Let's compare the worldly things we might want right now to who our Creator is:

The World Has...	And God...
Imperfect girlfriends/boyfriends	Is the perfect friend
Popularity in school	Is heard of by everyone
Success in life	Created all existence
Momentary happiness	Will never die

We think we have an idea of things such as perfection, beauty and love. But God surpasses these things infinitely.

- He IS perfection
- He IS beauty
- He IS love

...and he wants to have a relationship with us! There is nothing greater than God, and if we can begin to see him this way, then we can begin to realize that there is nothing in existence that can compare to what we can have with our Lord.

With God, you have the power to break free from your sinful nature. God will not allow us to be tempted beyond what we can bear (1 Corinthians 10:13). And we do not live on bread alone, but on the very words of God (Matthew 4:4). If we open the Bible and devote ourselves to the teachings of Jesus, we will realize just how amazing the truth is, and we won't find anything better!

1. Do you find it difficult or easy to be honest with yourself about where you are right now? Why?

2. How can identifying your desires and realizing your thoughts help you be honest about where you are?

3. After reading this chapter and seeing the need to assess your current spiritual state, where do you honestly believe yourself to be right now?

4. Write down your response to this: "When I came to the conclusion that none of my worldly desires would get me to heaven and none of them would last forever, I realized I had to work to get my heart to where it needed to be."

5. Do you ever wonder if you are turning into a couch potato as I was? If so, what do you think could turn this around for you?

KEEPING IT REAL
A Carefully Crafted Front

It was a couple of weeks into my sentence of being grounded for the next millennium and a half. I went to midweek service, and since there was no teen class that night, I just hung out in the hallway with my friends Armando, Ryan and Adam. All of us had been disciples for at least a couple of years at this point.

Our conversation was far from spiritual—I think skateboards and video games were about as deep as we got. We sat there wasting time until our new teen leader, Frank, came up. He had already been a great help and example to us, but he was about to catch all four of us by complete surprise.

"How are you guys doing tonight?" he asked.

"Not bad," one or two of us responded.

"Okay, but how are you actually doing?"

Uh-oh. Frank wanted to dig a little deeper. All of us knew what he meant, but none of us responded. Frank was doing something that we hadn't done for each other in months: He was trying to find out how we were doing spiritually.

"You guys want to go into the back office and shoot the breeze?" he asked.

We all looked at each other, then back at Frank.

"I guess, yeah."

"Sure."

"Why not?"

"Okay."

So we all went with Frank to the office room to "hang out." Needless to say, Frank had no intention of hanging out and shooting the breeze. He wanted to know how we were all holding up spiritually. Were we blazing the spiritual trail at our high schools or hanging on for dear life? Since Frank was still fairly new to our teen ministry, he needed to know what he was dealing with; but more important, he deeply and genuinely cared about each of us and our walk with God.

Armando, Ryan, Adam and I were the closest of friends, and we spent a lot of time together. We slept over at each other's houses. We were the first on the list for each other's birthday parties. We had even been involved in each other's Bible studies before we were baptized. We knew each other very well, but we were soon to find out that each of us had been putting up such clever, well-constructed spiritual fronts that only Jesus and maybe Superman's laser vision could have seen through.

Eventually, the spotlight turned on me.

Frank said, "So Drew, why exactly did you get grounded by your parents anyway?"

My eyes almost popped out of my head. "Who, me?"

"No, the other Drew. Yeah you, dork," Frank teased.

"Well, um, if you guys must know, I've been going out to parties for the last few months and my parents found out. So they grounded me royally for it."

I waited for my friends to rebuke me or tell me what a sinner I was, but all I got from them was, "Oh, that stinks."

That's all you have to say? I thought to myself. Why didn't any of my friends act surprised that I had been partying this whole time? I was confused at first, but it didn't take long for all of it to make sense.

Frank started a discussion about my spiritual life (or lack thereof). Everyone else seemed uncomfortable, and I didn't know why until Adam spoke up.

"Well, I've been going to parties too; I just haven't told anyone," he said. "But I know it's wrong. I know the stuff I've been doing at these parties is wrong. But now it feels good to get open about it because I need to act like a disciple again."

"You're right, and I've been partying with my friends at school too," said Ryan.

"Yeah, me too," admitted Armando.

I still don't really understand how Frank pulled it off, but by the end of our time of "shooting the breeze" that night at midweek service, Frank had brought out things about each of my "closest friends" that I had absolutely no idea were going on. We realized that all of us had been going to parties with our own friends at school. (Russell, my friend from church who had been my partner in crime, wasn't there that night. He actually stopped coming to church soon after.)

My confessions that night explained a lot to the guys, and their confessions explained a lot to me. All of us were busy fooling each other, and all of us were busy being fooled.

Choosing the Right Friendships

It is no secret: Our friendships, especially in our teen years, can shape our thoughts and decisions more than any other relationship, including our parents. I certainly had friends at school who led me astray. But at times, ironically, it was my friends at church who led me the furthest away from God! I let my Christian friends influence my views on Christ, discipleship and the church because I respected their views on spiritual things. I often looked to their spirituality as a reference point for how well I was doing; if they were struggling, I became lazy spiritually because they weren't spurring me on. But if they were doing well, I knew I had to kick it in gear, or else I would be the one who looked like he was struggling and who was left out of the "cool spiritual club."

Now don't get me wrong, I am grateful in the most profound way for the impact that my closest friends in the teen ministry had on my spiritual life. I would certainly have chosen the same friends again if I were to go back and live it all a second time. However, it was all too easy for us to lose track of the important role that we played in each other's spiritual walks. All of us were struggling spiritually, and none of us went to each other for help. All of us were losing interest in God, and none of us was talking about it.

Keep the teens talking about their relationship w/ God, good or bad

One of the main reasons this occurred was that none of us wanted to stop living our double lives at school, and at the same time, none of us wanted to be outcasts at church for falling too deep into sin. The result was that each of us put up a "don't ask, don't tell" front. We fooled each other into believing that we were doing well enough to not need any spiritual guidance, and up until that night at midweek service our strategies had been working perfectly. It wasn't until Frank challenged us to confront the reality of our spiritual condition that we all realized we needed to get back on the right path with God and with each other.

Keeping It Real

There are a number of great references in the Bible to the types of friends God expects us to look for. Proverbs 18:24 says, "A man of many companions may come to ruin, but there is a friend who sticks closer than a brother." The Bible says in Jeremiah 17:9, "The heart is deceitful above all things." We need people in our lives to tell us what we need to hear. If your closest friends know you and love you, your heart won't be able to deceive them the way it can deceive you!

What do our teens need to hear?

I believe that the most important thing you should look for in a friend, especially a Christian friend, is that they will be honest with you and challenge you to be honest with yourself. Friends who make you feel good about yourself and tell you everything you want to hear might be easy to hang around, but they won't help you make it to heaven. You must have people around you who will not allow you to deceive yourself.

My Christian friends and I were each in a rough place spiritually, and although none of us was in a place to preach, we could have at least been true friends to each other. We could have asked simple, heartfelt questions. I look back on that time and I think how much it would have helped if I had just asked Ryan, Armando or Adam, "Are you as unhappy about going to church as I am? Do you think it's okay that we feel this way? What should we do?" But this never happened because I wasn't honest with myself, and I wasn't working to help my friends be honest with themselves either.

That night at church, with Frank's help, we were finally open with each other, and a wonderful rebirth occurred in each of our hearts. We all graduated from high school firm in our walk with God.

Finding a Mentor

As much as our friends can affect our decisions, for better or for worse, there are limits to their influence. This is because our peers are going through the same stage of life, trying to figure out the same things we are. We can't look at their lives and gain vision for our own future, because we are both at the same point in life. There are certain areas of life that can only be influenced by someone older, someone we look up to and respect.

When I was a young disciple, this person for me was a guy named Jeremy. I grew up knowing Jeremy because our families were good friends. When I was really young, I thought he was the coolest guy in the world because he was in high school and he had all the best video games at his house (I didn't have any at the time). I loved going over to his house to hang out with him and play video games.

When I entered the teen ministry, Jeremy was my teen leader.

He used to invite me and a few of the other guys over to his place to read scriptures and also to just hang out and have fun. He helped me figure out what to do when I liked a girl at school or at church. When I did something stupid, he helped me to see how I could have been smarter. When I did something smart, he encouraged me and made me feel important.

I always greatly respected Jeremy's walk with God and also the way he went about his academic career. When I was in middle school and early high school, Jeremy was just finishing college. When I would hang out with him, I would think in the back of my mind, "This is a guy I want to be like when I am in college." Jeremy had a lot of things going on in his life, but he always made time to hang out with me and talk about how my life was going. I couldn't even list all the ways his influence helped me! It is so important as a follower of Jesus to have an older friend who can mentor you and help you grow. I was very fortunate to have a guy like Jeremy in my life.

After Jeremy finished college, he got married and moved to a different city. Because of all of the help he had given me, I understood the importance of having a mentor in my life, and so even as I've gotten older myself, I still make it a point to find older friends I can learn from. I always try to have a mentor in my life.

Pay It Forward

When I was a senior in high school (after the mess that was my junior year), I had the privilege of being a camp counselor at my church's preteen camp. There were two young guys in my cabin named Matthew and Julio. During that preteen camp, we bonded with each other, and I knew that God wanted me to be a "Jeremy" to them. After that camp, I stayed friends with Matthew and Julio, and helped them in any way I could. By the grace of God they were both baptized and are now walking with Christ on their high school campuses.

One Sunday during my senior year, Jeremy came back to church to visit his family, and I went up to him and told him that I was following in his footsteps by helping the guys in the youth ministry as a mentor. Telling this to Jeremy gave me so much joy because I remembered how much I had wanted to be like him, and there I was, helping other young men just as he had helped me!

Sometimes I wonder where I would be now if I hadn't had any mentors like Jeremy in my life. Or even worse, what if I'd had a mentor, but that person was someone who did not love God, someone who had influenced me in worldly ways? The chances of me still being a Christian today would be slim.

The Three Amigos

I have a philosophy, based on the Scriptures, about the types of relationships we all need as disciples. (And this principle holds true for the other roles we play in life: student, athlete, employee...)

There are three types of people we want to have in our lives:

- Paul
- Timothy
- Jonathan

One of the deepest mentoring relationships we find in the New Testament is the friendship between Paul and Timothy. If you read 1 and 2 Timothy, you see Paul giving all kinds of advice to Timothy. Paul loves Timothy very much, and Paul is like a father or older brother to Timothy. On the flip side, we know that Timothy looked up to Paul greatly and listened to every word he said. In a letter to the church in Corinth, Paul wrote,

> For this reason I am sending to you Timothy, my son whom I love, who is faithful in the Lord. He will remind you of my way of life in Christ Jesus, which agrees with what I teach everywhere in every church. (1 Corinthians 4:17)

Finally, there is Jonathan. Jonathan was the son of Saul, the king. He should have been next in line for his father's throne, but God chose David. Amazingly Jonathan didn't become jealous of David; instead, he became his closest friend. Before David became king he was a track star—that is, he had to run around all over the place so that King Saul wouldn't kill him! During this very difficult time in David's life, Jonathan stayed by his friend's side even though it was his own father who was trying to kill David!

At David's most desperate hour, when he didn't know how he was going to get away from Saul, Jonathan said to David, "Whatever you want me to do, I'll do for you" (1 Samuel 20:4). With Jonathan's help, David escaped and stayed alive; eventually, he became king of Israel. There was a loyalty in the friendship between David and Jonathan that made two ordinary guys as close as brothers.

What About You?

Think about these things:

Do you have a Paul in your life...
  - Someone you can go to for honest advice—advice that might be difficult to hear sometimes, but that you actually listen to?
  - Someone you greatly respect and admire, someone you want to be like some day?

Do you have a Timothy in your life...
  - Someone you can be an older brother or sister to?
  - Someone you care about and want to mentor?

Do you have any Jonathans in your life...

- Someone who sticks as close as a brother or sister?
- Someone who is right there with you in the battles of life?
- Someone you can help and at the same time receive help from?
- Someone who is not necessarily going to give you a whole bunch of advice, but who is in the same walk of life and knows what you are going through?

Back at the church office that night, my friends and I didn't realize it, but Frank was being our Paul. Sadly, we had been doing a very bad job at being each other's Jonathans. And we were certainly in no place to influence some of the younger guys in the teen ministry who could have used our help. But thankfully, God worked through Frank, and each of us was able to get going on the right track again, helping each other in our walk with God.

GET REAL

1. Is it true that as a teen your friends can shape your thoughts and decisions more than any other relationship, including your parents? If so, why do you think this is?
2. On a scale of 1 to 10, how real are you with your friends in the church? What changes do you need to make in this area?
3. Do you have a Jeremy (or a Paul) in your life to mentor you? If so, are you taking advantage of the help they can give you? If not, who could you ask to play this role in your life?
4. If you are an older teen and you are already a disciple, who are you helping and encouraging spiritually? Why is it important for your own growth for you to play this role in someone's life?

KEEPING IT REAL
I Don't Want to Go to Hell

Allow me to backtrack a bit to the summer before my eighth grade year. I went to the annual Los Angeles International Church of Christ teen summer camp at California Lutheran University. These camps were an amazing experience. All the teens there were always excited because of the atmosphere and the fun, but also because we were surrounded by a bunch of people our age who were interested in God to some degree.

This was also at a time when our church was experiencing an amazing growth in the teen ministry. These camps were a different experience than normal high school life because at camp it wasn't weird to be a Christian. It was actually just the opposite: You could feel like an outcast if you weren't involved in the spiritual atmosphere like everyone else.

That summer, I sat in one of the morning lessons, and the speaker's message was simple: It was about hell. As the speaker expounded on the gruesome and horrifying imagery that is found in the Bible about hell and eternal damnation, these ideas were pressed with great effect onto my heart and mind. I was unsettled in the worst way by the idea of one day entering through the "gates of Hades." I walked away from this message, and for the first time in my life, I concluded that if I died that day I would not be justified before God.

I had never looked at life from this angle before. I had grown up going to church and knowing a lot about what the Bible taught about hell, but I had never considered the possibility that I was ever in danger of actually going there. I returned home from camp very afraid. I approached my youth ministry leaders about studying the Bible, and the process of my becoming a disciple began.

CHAPTER 7

Your Decision to Study the Bible

Most of the pressure that Kingdom Kids feel stems from other people's hopes that they will be saved. Everyone around them at church—parents, friends, friends of friends—hopes that they will decide to study the Bible, decide to become a disciple, be baptized, and successfully live the Christian life. We know that this is what God wants for our life. And our parents long for the day when they see us saved. Nothing hurts a Christian parent more than the idea of their son or daughter not making it to heaven.

I grew up never seriously doubting the existence of God, heaven, Satan or hell. Certainly there were times when I wavered, but I never turned my back on the teachings of the Bible. So when I finally reached the age when I started to feel responsible for my own sin, I couldn't offer a good reason why I shouldn't begin studying the Bible in order to become a Christian. I knew that I was a sinner in the eyes of God; I knew that my sins were not yet forgiven, and I knew I didn't want to go to hell.

No one ever directly pressured me to study the Bible. The people around me understood that teens, just like anyone else, need to be able to make the decision on their own. My parents never had talks with me about how they would be disappointed in me if I didn't become a disciple. They never said that I would be a bad son if I didn't decide to follow Christ. They never said things like this, but I felt the pressure nonetheless. I knew in my heart that if I didn't decide to become a disciple, my parents would be devastated. I also knew that if I didn't become a disciple, I wouldn't be able to relate to my closest friends at church who were all starting to study the Bible and prepare themselves for baptism.

Making It Yours

When it comes to beginning Bible studies to help them become Christians, Kingdom Kids must ask themselves, "Why do I want to do this? Why do I actually want to study the Bible?" Everyone who seeks God should ask himself or herself this question, but this is especially important for the Kingdom Kid. Because they have grown up going to church, they know all the right answers. They know what they are "supposed" to think and "supposed" to want; they even know all the arguments for why a person should be baptized into Jesus to become a Christian!

But superficial knowledge doesn't matter. Interestingly, because Kingdom Kids already understand so much about the Bible, they are the least likely to actually understand themselves—to know the true reason why they want to consider baptism.

When someone has lived without God their whole life, it is usually obvious to them why they want to study the Bible to become a Christian. It is obvious to them because life as a Christian is far different from the worldly life they have known, and they want to be a part of this new lifestyle they have found. It is obvious because they can more easily identify the sins that are keeping them from having a relationship with God. These things are not as obvious to the Kingdom Kid because their external life probably won't change as dramatically after they are baptized.

Think about it: Once you decide to become a disciple of Jesus and are baptized into him, you will still be part of the same social circle at church. Your schedule won't change that much— you'll go to the same church events you did before. And you will still live inside the same boundaries, with the Bible as your guide. It's your *heart* that needs to change.

As a Kingdom Kid, you are going to have to think long and hard about why you really want to study the Bible. It is hard to do, but you must put aside your family, friends and every other source of pressure. You must clear your mind of all this and consider for yourself why *you* want to follow Jesus for the rest of your life.

Getting the Chance to Experience the World

One problem that many Kingdom Kids have is they feel like they need to experience life and understand what the world has to offer before they give everything to Christ. Although I wish I could sugarcoat my response, the truth is that if you have this attitude, then you probably aren't ready to become a disciple.

The apostle John says,

> Do not love the world or anything in the world. If anyone loves the world, the love of the Father is not in him. For everything in the world—the cravings of sinful man, the lust of his eyes and the boasting of what he has and does—comes not from the Father but from the world. The world and its desires pass away, but the man who does the will of God lives forever. (1 John 2:15–17)

The Bible teaches that you must hate sin and love righteousness, but if you spend your high school and college years wishing you were living the worldly life, then clearly you do not hate sin! If you really do wish to go out and experience what it feels like to be part of the world, when you graduate from high school and move out of your parents' house, you will have all the space you need away from home and church to do whatever it is you want to do.

However, keep in mind that you will *not* have the freedom to judge your own soul; that power is God's alone. He explains clearly in his word (which you have had the *privilege* of learning your entire life) that the soul who indulges in the sinful nature will not inherit the kingdom of heaven. I do not present this fact to scare you back into submission to the teachings of Christ, but because it is the truth.

A Blessing?

If you are stuck in this position—wishing you could experience the world, but feeling too guilty to really go after it—let's be honest: You're in a difficult and painful place! No one wants to be caught between two worlds—curious about a sinful life they've never known, but too afraid to try it because of the possibility of hell and everlasting guilt. No one wants to be forced to choose which way to go. Either way, it feels like you are leaving a part of your heart out on the table.

If you choose to remain a Christian, you worry that you might regret not experiencing all that the world has to offer. But if you venture out into the world, you risk the possibility of missing the grace of God. Ultimately, nothing anyone says is going to make this choice easier for you because these are matters of your heart. However, looking at it from a different perspective might help you realize that this period of limbo, when you are weighing out whether to pursue the world or remain faithful to God, is actually a blessing.

Okay, I bet some of you are thinking, *What?! Drew's really lost it here. He's saying it's GOOD that I'm struggling with wanting the world. Maybe I should put this book down and run the other way.* But keep reading; I'm not done!

In the book of Genesis, we read about two of the most sinful communities described in the Bible. God tells Lot and his wife to flee Sodom and Gomorrah before he destroys the cities, so they do.

Lot and his wife understand God's wrath against Sodom and Gomorrah, but at the same time, they have fallen in love with the life they had experienced there. We pick up the story in Genesis 19:23–27:

> By the time Lot reached Zoar, the sun had risen over the land. Then the LORD rained down burning sulfur on Sodom and Gomorrah—from the LORD out of the heavens. Thus he overthrew those cities and the entire plain, including all those living in the cities—and also the vegetation in the land. But Lot's wife looked back, and she became a pillar of salt.

Lot's wife had fallen so much in love with sin that she could not bring her heart to let go of what she had in Sodom and Gomorrah, and it killed her...literally. If Lot had not led his family to live in Sodom and Gomorrah, they would not have been exposed to the sins there, and maybe their hearts would have stayed close to God. But instead, their eyes were opened to the pleasures of sin, and Lot's wife could not let go—when the place was destroyed, she looked back, and God knew where her heart truly was.

As Kingdom Kids, we have had the blessing of parents and youth leaders who have led us away from Sodom and Gomorrah. They have protected us from the sinful influences of the world. They have sheltered us from seeing, doing and experiencing many things. But if we go out into the world and pursue a life of sin, the scary thing is that we may fall too far and our hearts may never want to let go of the world. Even if we want to come back, our hearts may be too hardened to make it.

As much as we hated being caught in the middle, we will *still* find ourselves in limbo! But this time, instead of our curiosity about the world pulling us away from God, we will be dealing with the opposite problem: trying to come back to God while we are chained, glued and nailed to the world by our own love of sin! I don't know about you, but that sounds like a horrible struggle to me. At that point, a little curiosity about a life you never knew will seem far better than living in slavery to sins that you cannot escape.

Very Real Consequences

The reality is that sin has consequences. We know that Jesus had to die on the cross to pay the debt for our sin. But think about this: *We pay some of the price of sin ourselves.* Even if we repent and receive forgiveness, some consequences remain. Once you lose your virginity, you can't have it back. Once you engage in sin, even when God "forgives and forgets," you can't erase your memory of it. If you hurt someone else or if you get hurt emotionally or physically, some wounds don't go completely away even when you are forgiven. The battle we fight against the world lasts a lifetime, and the more we sin, the more costs we have to pay.

A good friend of mine in high school went through an intense struggle with the world. She is a faithful disciple today, but her teen years were tough. I asked her to write down her story so that I could share it with you in this chapter. It's a great example of the struggle that many teens go through when we battle our desire to experience "happiness and freedom" in the world:

The main thing that I struggled with in the world was dating relationships. In middle school, all of my friends had boyfriends except me. At one point I really liked a boy who ended up dating my friend instead. By the time I got to high school, I felt as if I had missed out on something.

My freshman year in high school I went to a school that none of my church friends went to. No one really knew who I was, so it was easy for me to create this new and popular persona. I made new friends who all had boyfriends, so once again l felt left out. No one at school ever pressured me into having a boyfriend, but because they all were dating it just made me feel like I was missing something.

At home, my parents (who are disciples) were against me dating a guy from school, but I felt I could get away with it if I took the right precautions. I dated two boys at my first high school. The next year I transferred to a different school and never spoke to those guys again.

At my new school, just like the last one, all of my new friends had boyfriends. This time they were taking things to a whole new level. They talked about their relationships going long-term and about marriage and things I did not really care about, but I felt that I needed to because of my friends. So I felt even more pressure to find the best boyfriend I could find.

By my senior year, I had dated boys from five different schools. I was becoming known for the boys I dated, who were usually elite athletes. In the process of dating all these guys, I lost my two best friends, who tried to advise me against dating so many boys. I was far too wrapped up in the security of fitting in. I completely ignored their advice, and our friendship faded because we had less to talk about.

Throughout high school, I was only ever in love with one boy, but he didn't want to date me until my senior year. Before then I really just dated guys because I felt I needed to fit in and do what girls were supposed to do to be cool. People at church frowned upon my decisions. I openly spoke against the dating advice that I was given in our youth group. Many people didn't agree with me, and my reputation was heavily damaged because of my choices.

When I finally did date that boy my senior year, he ended up cheating on me, and most of the people I knew found out about it. I was crushed. This experience taught me a lot about relationships away from God; I was finally starting to realize why my youth ministers felt the way they did about dating guys who don't love God. They weren't just trying to restrict me; they were trying to protect me!

I know now what a real dating relationship looks like and what it is designed to do, which is to build one another up in purity and help each other get to heaven. It was hard for me to see this in high school, especially when all of my closest friends were in the world and didn't have God's desires on their hearts. Through it all, God always had a plan for me, and even though it hurt, he let my heart get broken my senior year so that I could wake up to the reality that a relationship with him was far more important than a relationship with any guy.

All those years I just wanted to be accepted, and I didn't realize that there were people who loved God and also loved me for who I was. Unfortunately, I have to live with the choices I made. Instead of being known by my old friends in my hometown for all of my sporting achievements, my personality or my grades, I am instead known for all of the boys I dated.

However, the friends I have today and the new people I meet know me for my love for God and for his people. At the end of my senior year, I was baptized into Christ. Although the life of a disciple may not be the easiest thing, God has always been there for me, so I put my faith in him.

I am grateful to my friend for sharing her story, which is a living example of this truth: It is so much better to choose life *now* instead of later (see Deuteronomy 30:11–20). Some of us think we can trick God: *Maybe I can try the world* (choose death) *now, and maybe later I'll repent* (choose life). But we don't realize it might be too late by then. And even if God does grant us repentance and a second chance, the price we pay will be high.

As you can see from my friend's story, she paid some heavy costs her senior year in high school, and even today her reputation is not a righteous one among her old friends. Fortunately, she received the wisdom and guidance to find the only relationship that will ever make her totally complete—but I'm sure she wishes her high school experience had been different, that she hadn't insisted on "learning the hard way."

If you are struggling with these decisions in your life, I want to ask you from the bottom of my heart to stop chasing the happiness that the world has to offer you. It is all self-focused, and it always leads to *more* struggling for *more* selfish things and the need for *more* happiness.

I promise that you won't feel left out and regretful when your worldly friends who *seem* happy start facing the high costs of sin in their lives. In fact, those people are probably going to need someone to pull them out of their struggles and back into a place of real comfort and true joy. You can be that person.

GET REAL

1. If you are not yet a Christian, do you feel some pressure from those around you to make a decision to follow Jesus and be baptized into him? How does that pressure come to you? How can you let go of what you feel to consider if you are ready to study the Bible with the intent to become a Christian?

2. Whether you are a Christian or not, share how you personally relate to the story that my friend shared. Do you feel that same pull that she felt? How does it affect you to hear some of the consequences of giving in to the worldly pull she felt?

3. Explain how the story of Lot's wife and the destruction of Sodom and Gomorrah can relate to teens struggling with the desire for the world.

KEEPING IT REAL
Forgiven—Before and After

It was September 1, 2001. I was fourteen years old. I came up out of the water in my parents' arms at a church retreat in Palm Springs, California, and my journey was complete; I had been baptized. It was a great weekend. I was on a spiritual high after finishing my Bible studies, getting baptized, and being around all of the disciples at the retreat. I was excited about my life as a disciple of Christ.

I returned from Palm Springs ready to take on the world! I had great quiet times that whole week. I was happy at church service. I had great talks with my parents and teen leaders. It was amazing. School started and I began my crusade at Hale Middle School. A few weeks passed, and it became more and more difficult to find time to read my Bible. I had a tougher time focusing on God and other people before myself. I grew more and more afraid to share the gospel on campus. Then it occurred to me: When I was baptized in Palm Springs, my journey hadn't been completed—it had just begun!

Once I came down off the spiritual high from my baptism and life went back to normal, I realized that my routine as a Christian wasn't really all that different from what it had been before. I still went to the same services; I still attended the same youth ministry events, and I still tried to read my Bible on my own, just as I had before. Certainly the expectations were now of a more serious nature than before, but the reality was that not a whole lot had changed!

But I was a disciple now...wasn't my life supposed to be radically different?

What was I doing wrong?

Radical Life Change

We know that conversion is meant to be a radical change: death to the old life, resurrection of the new. But this process can feel less dramatic for "good kids" who have spent a lifetime pursuing God on some level. Perhaps you are familiar with the "Seeking God Study"—the Bible study designed to help inspire people to more diligently pursue a walk with God. This is a great Bible study, but how can we seek any further for a God who has been brought to us every day since we were old enough to pray for our own food? How can we seek any further for a God whom we have already sought for years?

When I look back at my own decision to be baptized and follow Jesus, I realize that my story is not as dramatic or exciting as some other conversion stories that I have heard. At times I've wished I had one of those jaw-dropping transformation stories: "Yeah, a year ago I was a drug addict wandering the streets, mugging old ladies. Then Jesus changed me, and now I lead a church!" Sometimes I have wondered: Am I less saved because my story isn't as dramatic? Of course not! My change—and your change—is just as real, but for Kingdom Kids, many of our changes happen on the inside.

Developing Our Own Convictions

A radical life transformation can and must happen, but it will happen in a different way for Kingdom Kids than for those who have not attended church their entire life. One of the most important changes we Kingdom Kids must make is this: We must develop our own convictions and not just "go through the motions."

You may be asking, "What are 'the motions,' and why should I not go through them?" "The motions" are the general activities, behaviors and habits that are expected of disciples. To "go through" these activities is to do them simply for the sake of doing them, without considering *why*. We go through the motions when we do Christian things without purpose. Some examples of this would be

- Reading the Bible without trying to get anything out of it.
- Going to church but falling asleep during the sermon.
- Praying but having your mind on many other things and not actually connecting with God.

The book of Acts talks about the noble character of the Bereans (Acts 17:11), who did not merely listen to the teachings of the apostles and accept them on the spot, but instead read the Scriptures themselves. They wanted to make sure that what they were being told to do matched up with the will of God. This is a great example of disciples who weren't going through the motions, but were working every day to strengthen their relationship with God.

Looking back, I can think of many times when I went through the motions of discipleship:

- At teen camps I felt totally inspired to grow closer to God, but much of this enthusiasm wore off once I was no longer in such a spiritual atmosphere.
- In my times with God, I would read a quick scripture and pray a quick prayer without really digging deep into the Word or my own heart.
- At church services I would sit and listen, but I wouldn't work to apply what I had heard to help me grow.
- I did things like go to church, pray and read my Bible without considering why I was doing them.

A lot of this happened because I was letting my "spiritual routine" take control of me instead of taking control of my routine. The problem is not that going to church influences us to do spiritual things; the problem is when we let church do the thinking *for* us, and we stop considering what we believe and why we believe it. This is dangerous because when you are outside of your church's supervision and in a setting where the ideas of God are not as popular, you will have to rely upon your own convictions. And if you have *no* convictions or *weak* convictions, you won't make it.

Why love God? Why love people? Why go to church? The only person's answers that matter are *yours*—not your parents', not your youth ministry leaders', not your church elders'—because it is *you* who will always be with you! You cannot allow yourself to just go through the motions, because you need to develop your own personal convictions. Your own answer to the important questions of the spiritual walk must, must, MUST be your own.

Understand Why

When you come to understand the "why" for all the things you do, that will be enough. You will no longer need people to tell you to go to church, read your Bible or be giving to others. Knowing the "why" will be all the motivation you need. Instead of praying a quick prayer and reading a quick scripture, you will actually desire to dig deep and discover something new about God. Instead of simply saying "amen" in the sermons because the rest of the crowd is saying it, you will have your own reasons why you can proclaim that amen.

A great lesson on the consequences of going through the motions is found in the book of 1 Samuel:

> Now the Israelites went out to fight against the Philistines. The Israelites camped at Ebenezer, and the Philistines at Aphek. The Philistines deployed their forces to meet Israel, and as the battle spread, Israel was defeated by the Philistines, who killed about four thousand of them on the battlefield. When the soldiers returned to camp, the elders of Israel asked, "Why did the LORD bring defeat upon us today before the Philistines? Let us bring the ark of the LORD's covenant from Shiloh, so that it may go with us and save us from the hand of our enemies."
>
> So the people sent men to Shiloh, and they brought back the ark of the covenant of the LORD Almighty, who is enthroned between the cherubim. And Eli's two sons, Hophni and Phinehas, were there with the ark of the covenant of God.
>
> When the ark of the LORD's covenant came into the camp, all Israel raised such a great shout that the ground shook. Hearing the uproar, the Philistines asked, "What's all this shouting in the Hebrew camp?"
>
> When they learned that the ark of the LORD had come into the camp, the Philistines were afraid. "A god has come into the camp," they said. "We're in trouble! Nothing like this has happened before. Woe to us! Who will deliver us from the hand of these mighty gods? They are the gods who struck the Egyptians with all kinds of plagues in the desert.

> Be strong, Philistines! Be men, or you will be subject to the
> Hebrews, as they have been to you. Be men, and fight!"
>   So the Philistines fought, and the Israelites were defeated
> and every man fled to his tent. The slaughter was very great;
> Israel lost thirty thousand foot soldiers. The ark of God was
> captured, and Eli's two sons, Hophni and Phinehas, died.
> (1 Samuel 4:1–11)

We find the Israelites under attack by the Philistines. Defeated
in the first battle, they immediately get confused about what is
going on. Interestingly, if you read a little earlier, in chapter
three verse one it says, "In those days the word of the Lord was
rare; there were not many visions." Nevertheless, despite the
lack of the presence of God's word in their lives, they still had
rituals and duties of faith that made them *feel* like they were
being good Israelites.

The ark had always been a great morale booster for the Israelites, and so when it arrived, it gave them hope because they
believed that the Spirit of God resided in the ark. Unfortunately,
simply going through the motions of bringing the ark into the
battle camp was not enough to hand them victory. During that
time God's word was rare, and this gave far less meaning to the
arrival of the ark. God knew where their hearts truly were, and
so his blessing did not go with them into battle. The Israelites
went into battle with false hope, and were defeated by the
Philistines.

This reminds me of the way I used to go through my spiritual
life. I would slowly slip away from my devotion to the Bible. I
would read it less; I would talk about it less, and I would be less
involved in other people's spiritual lives. Without realizing it, I
trimmed my discipleship down to simply going to church meetings and having a brief time with God here and there that had
no influence on my actions for the rest of the day.

When difficult times came around and I struggled spiritually, I became confused about what was going on and why God wasn't delivering me from my struggles. I thought I was doing okay as a disciple! I was going to church, and I was spending a little time with God every day. I thought I was being a good Christian. So why wasn't I winning my spiritual battles? The truth was that God hadn't distanced himself from me; I had distanced myself from God.

In reality, the word of the Lord was rare in my life, just as it had been for the Israelites in 1 Samuel.

- I read the Scriptures, but I wasn't applying them.
- I went to church, but I was focused on myself instead of on how I could help people in the fellowship.
- I prayed, but I didn't put my heart into it.

I had been going through the motions and I had no idea that I had fallen so far.

Routine and Focus

I'll say it again: You must take control of your routine before your routine takes control of you. Our daily routine is one of the most crucial aspects of our discipleship, and it must be worthy of the calling we have received as disciples. I look back on my decision to study the Bible, and I am perfectly happy that I made the decision to be a disciple. This decision led me to where I am today, and for that I am truly grateful. But I also look back on it all, and I am a little perplexed at how little changed in my daily life after I was baptized:

- I had the same friends.
- I went to the same places.
- I did the same things.
- I still lived at home and the rules were still the same.
- I was still Drew.

Considering the glorious fact that my sins were forgiven, my day-to-day life didn't change all that much, because I had already been living the lifestyle of a disciple in many ways. But what *did* change was my heart and the reasons I followed my routines: My spiritual disciplines (like reading my Bible, going to church, spending time with other Christians) became things I wanted to do in order to please God and draw closer to him, instead of things I was "supposed" to do.

Even though my heart changed when I became a Christian, it took (and still takes) a lot of work to *keep* my heart and my focus in the right place.

It is our nature as human beings to develop routines for how we live our lives. The danger here is that when we set up a routine, it becomes easy to lose track of the purpose behind what we are doing. For example, I eat breakfast every morning before I leave home. Sometimes I am not even hungry; I just eat because it is part of my routine. Sometimes I am so zoned out that I don't even realize what I am doing—just the other day I poured cereal into my half-full water glass, for crying out loud!

We have already discussed what it means to go through the motions spiritually. It is one thing to go to church out of habit, and it is something totally different to go to church with purpose. Think about it—human beings tend to zone out. This is why there are so many car accidents: People zone out while they drive. People zone out while they are in class. People zone out at work. You have probably zoned out a few times while reading this book. *But you cannot zone out in your Christian life!* What would church be like if the preacher zoned out in the middle of his sermon and forgot what he was saying?

It is no less important to God that you stay focused in your spiritual walk too. The minute you begin zoning out in your Christianity is the minute you become a target for Satan.

Even though I had already been doing many of "the right things" before I was baptized, I still had plenty of stuff to change inside, because as Christians, we are supposed to live *the way Jesus lived*, not the way we ourselves *think* Christians are expected to live.

The most important things to Jesus, above any religious event or ritual, were his relationships with God and with other people. Though he certainly had his own routines, his focus was always on deepening his connection with those around him. If we add this focus to our daily routine, we will be well on our way to living as Jesus did.

Self-Evaluation

You must consider: How is your daily, weekly and monthly routine different today than it was before you started studying the Bible? Is your heart and attitude different in the things you do? How is your routine more focused on God and people than it was before?

- Do you watch the same amount of television when you could be spending more time with God?
- Do you spend the same amount of time just having fun with your friends without really getting to know them?
- Do you read your Bible more than you used to, or in a deeper way, with more focus and eagerness?
- Do you spend more time trying to help people than you used to?

Our lives must change once we decide to make Jesus Lord. Changing your routine and changing the level of focus you have for God and for the people around you are radical steps in the right direction.

My Third Conversion: Humility

People who did not grow up immersed in our church culture must make radical changes in their character and lifestyle when they become Christians. Many of their changes have to do with leaving their former way of life and becoming part of the Christian culture. The church calendar alone calls for radical change! A new busy schedule—full of Bible studies, Sunday services, devotionals and times with other Christians—is a big adjustment.

But Kingdom Kids live the Christian schedule long before we study the Bible, so as I've said before, the changes for us may be less obvious. Because we've spent our whole lives learning to live the way Christian kids are supposed to live, we have a lot of the right behaviors down. We need help transforming our *insides* more than our *outsides*. A lot of our character flaws are not as easy to spot, and although we come to Christ wholeheartedly, we can miss out on truly transforming our character.

Many young teens spend time doing "character studies" from the Bible to help prepare them to become Christians. They may study godly character traits or people in the Bible, in order to develop specific pictures of what a Christian character looks like. Studies like these are a stepping-stone intended to help Kingdom Kids get in touch with the meaning of character, but we can still miss the *heart* of Bible studies like these. Simply going through the character studies and memorizing the Scriptures is not going to be enough to transform us.

We Kingdom Kids need to be seriously cut by our character flaws and learn to crucify our sinful nature so we can be made holy by Christ. Character studies can begin this process, but it is up to us to make the internal change; the studies aren't going to do the work for us.

Kingdom Kids who are baptized at an early age, as I was, usually go through a second conversion later in life. I am a strong testament to this. In fact, I have had three "conversions"! My first two you already know about from what you have read in this book so far:

- At fourteen I studied the Bible, made a decision to be a disciple and was baptized. Here I dealt with my faith, sins and my need for forgiveness. This is when I was first converted.
- At eighteen I learned how to find real happiness in my relationship with God (I will share specifically about this in the "Keeping It Real" section for chapter 9).
- At twenty-two I discovered the importance of having real humility in my character.

At each of these stages in my life, another slice of my heart was converted to Christ. Growing up through high school and college, the one thing I lacked more than anything else was humility. You may struggle with a different aspect of your character—everyone has their own issues—but my primary struggle was definitely pride. I always used to think I was better than people. I didn't necessarily walk around consciously thinking to myself, "I am better than him, and that guy over there is not even close to being as spiritual as I am, and that girl over there just doesn't get it the way I do," but these thoughts were in the back of my mind. I never dealt with these thoughts because I never admitted that they were there.

Through most of my college years, I didn't really listen to anybody who tried to disciple me, including my campus ministry leaders. Although I had "disciplers," I didn't let anyone teach or train me. Although I had "peers," I often felt one step above the people around me. It was really sad, because this lack of humility kept me from really getting to know people.

God had to seriously discipline the pride out of my life. If I had just been honest with myself about this part of my character, I would have humbled myself sooner. Instead, God did it for me:

- For a couple years, I battled depression.
- I distanced myself from my closest friends.
- I ruined the friendship I had with a girl in the campus ministry who I wanted to date.
- I couldn't find my role in the fellowship.
- I almost left my church.

Finally, at one of the lowest points in my life spiritually, I realized that my problem was the lack of humility in my character. I began to seek help and to change, and God showed me how much he loves humility by beginning to bless me in areas of my life I thought I would never be blessed in. My friendships started to go deeper than they had been in a very long time. God gave me amazing opportunities for my career when I finished college. And best of all, I began to get closer to God than I had ever been in my life.

It's About Who You Are

As disciples, it can be very easy to get caught up in all that we need to do. This is partly why it's so easy to start going through the motions in our spiritual routines. Most of the spiritual disciplines that we are expected to do are good for us and should be on our hearts. Habits like spending consistent time with God, reading the Bible, and attending meetings of the church body are important to the success of our personal walk with God and the closeness of the church family. However, our focus on these actions can all too often cause us to have a slightly skewed impression of what spirituality is.

Among all of the tasks and expectations of Christianity, we may begin to think, "If I do *this*, *this* and *this*, then I will feel like I am doing well spiritually." Although it might be true that a spiritual person would do *this, this* and *this* (fill in the blanks), just doing those things does not automatically make us spiritual people. I firmly believe that our actions do not determine who we are; instead, who we are determines our actions. For example, Jesus was the Son of God and he loved people more than himself—that is who he was. All of his desires and actions came from who he was deep down inside. So...

- When Satan tempted Jesus, he wouldn't succumb because he wasn't that person.
- When Pilate tried to convince Jesus to speak in his own defense at his trial, he would not speak because he wasn't that person.
- When the blind and deaf sought Jesus' help in the streets, he helped them because he *was* that person.

Everything Jesus did stemmed from who he was. Asking yourself the question "Is all of this really who I am?" forces you to take your definition of spirituality deeper.

Am I doing these spiritual things because I am a person who loves God? Or am I doing these things because I am a person who wants to please my friends, parents and other disciples? I may be motivated to study my Bible now, but what about when I leave home and find myself in the freshman dorm on a Friday night? What will happen when I am no longer so entrenched in the church culture that has made it so comfortable for me to pursue a spiritual life? Who will I be when I am by myself?

If your freedom has led you to become a disciple of Christ, and this is who you really are, you need not worry. Granted, you will not be perfect. You will have your good days and your bad days, but you will not give up the fight, because it is your identity to be a person who follows God to the end of your life.

God is the one who measures spirituality. Not your parents, not you, not your ministry leader, not any person on the planet. Only God. All too often we get so caught up in meeting our own expectations or other people's expectations that we forget *God's* expectations, which are the most loving and most beneficial of all.

Who We Want to Be

The person we are trying to be like is Jesus. This is no secret, but we must look at who Jesus was and what drove him if we are going to understand who we need to be and what needs to motivate us. As Kingdom Kids, because we have been going to church for such a long time, it is easy to let all the complexities of the Christian "to-do list" cloud our view of what it means to be spiritually successful. This is why it is so important for us to return to the basics of God's plan for mankind.

> One of the teachers of the law came and heard them debating. Noticing that Jesus had given them a good answer, he asked him, "Of all the commandments, which is the most important?"
> "The most important one," answered Jesus, "is this: 'Hear, O Israel, the Lord our God, the Lord is one. Love the Lord your God with all your heart and with all your soul and with all your mind and with all your strength.' The second is this: 'Love your neighbor as yourself.' There is no commandment greater than these." (Mark 12:28–31)

I love this scripture so much because it always takes me back to the essence of what God expects from every one of his children: *to love him and each other with all of our hearts.* This is what God created us for. Not to be popular at school or have a good career or make a lot of money. Not even to have a quiet time every day of our life, just for the sake of having a quiet time. God created us for relationships. He created us to have a relationship with him and to have relationships with other people.

God's two greatest commands are to love him and love other people. The way we show our love for God is by loving the people around us. This is how God measures spirituality. He doesn't measure it by

- How many books of the Bible you have read.
- How many people you have shared your faith with today.
- Your attendance record at Sunday church service.
- How many hours you spend in prayer and fasting.
- How much money you gave for contribution last Sunday.

God measures spirituality by the amount of love he sees in your heart for him and the people around you. This is the type of people we want to be: Christians who live our lives out of love. The beauty of this is that real love for God and for people will naturally spur us on to do the things a true disciple of Jesus would do because we *want* to. We will spend time with God because we love him. We will go to church because we love our church family. We will help the needy because we love them.

The deeper we look into our own hearts and intentions, the more we will understand why we are doing the things we are doing and who we are as people. When you are serving God or other people it is helpful to ask yourself questions such as

- Am I doing this because I was told to or because I want to serve?
- Am I sharing my faith out of obligation or because I love the person I'm sharing with?
- Am I reading my Bible right now because I think I should (and others think I should) or because I love God's word?

Asking yourself why you do the things that you do will help you understand where your heart is. We are striving to be people of love. That is who Jesus was, and who we can also be.

Don't Overanalyze

Now I should probably pause here and take a moment to address a different kind of Kingdom Kid: those who always feel guilty and never feel like they do enough. This chapter isn't as much for you as it is for hard-hearted knuckleheads like me. I'm not trying to make you paranoid about your motivations all the time—you could drive yourself crazy if you're always analyzing whether you're doing things for the right reasons!—but I am trying to remind us all to take our discipleship deeper.

It's good to check your heart every now and again (not every second of every day!), to make sure you're doing things out of love, not out of legalism or habit.

I hope this chapter will inspire you to deepen your understanding of your faith and your heart. To do "spiritual things" because you love God and you *want* to do them, not because you've been taught to do them your whole life. To love people because you really love them, not because you are supposed to. That's the life of a Christian. That's radical change that lasts a lifetime.

1. Even though a Kingdom Kid's conversion story might not be as "dramatic" as someone else's story, why is it just as valid? What radical "inside" changes does a Kingdom Kid make when Jesus becomes Lord?
2. What does it mean to "just go through the motions" spiritually speaking? Do you catch yourself doing this? If so, how do you reconnect with what you believe and why?
3. Explain why the following statement simplifies our spiritual lives: "This is what God expects from every one of

his children: to love him and each other with all of our hearts." How did Jesus live this out?

4. Write in your own words what you think is meant by this statement: "Our actions do not determine who we are; instead, who we are determines our actions."

KEEPING IT REAL
Reconnecting with God

Finally, the end of my junior year in high school had come. It had been my roughest year as a Christian. I had been caught partying by my parents and grounded for the full school year. I had found out that my closest friends at church were living as much of a double life as I had been living. I didn't know how to get back on my feet spiritually. I was getting help from my teen leaders and other people, but something had to happen within my own heart. I had to find a way to become content in my walk with God. I had to find a way to be happy with my decision to continue living as a disciple because I knew in my heart that it was the truth. I also knew that the world had nothing better to offer me.

I began the summer in limbo. I knew I wanted to get back into the swing of things spiritually, but my heart was still confused. Summer teen camp was coming soon, and to be honest, I wasn't looking forward to it that much. However, I still went and decided that I would try to make the best of it. All of the lessons and activities at the camp were great, and I had a fun time, but the best part of camp was what happened inside my heart. Something happened that sparked a whole new beginning in my walk with God.

On the second day of camp, I woke up early in the morning and couldn't get back to sleep. I lay there in my bunk for a good fifteen minutes before I decided to go out and read some scriptures and pray. This was out of the ordinary for me at camp because I always tried to have quiet times with other people, but that day something compelled me to go alone. So before the sun even rose, I got up, left my cabin, and went out to pray.

When I prayed, I was extremely honest with myself and with God about where I was spiritually and where I wanted to be. I was able to express things to God that I had never expressed to him: all that I had been struggling with that past year in school, all my anxieties about not enjoying the Christian life, all my fears about the pressure from church and my parents. All of this came out in my time with God, and I was able to connect with him in a way that I had never connected before.

By the time I was finished, the sun was up and it was almost time for breakfast. I knew that things would be different from then on in my spiritual walk. I knew that I was ready to once again live the way that Jesus calls his disciples to live.

Getting Back Up

Considering all of the pressure and spiritual expectations that were put on me as a Kingdom Kid, it was almost unavoidable that I would begin feeling like I had to be perfect. In the back of my mind, I often felt like any misstep in my walk was absolutely unacceptable. My wild imagination had me believing that somehow my sins would cause an uproar in my own family that would send a shockwave through church, setting in motion the apocalypse! I would be excommunicated from the church; God would turn away from me, and I would be condemned to hell for all eternity.

Obviously this is a bit of an exaggeration, but my point is that I was terrified of the consequences of my actions and the ripple effect they would have on my reputation in the church. I could not commit this or that sin, or make this or that decision because people would find out, and that just wasn't an option for me. I couldn't bear the thought of letting people down. In my mind, it would have done horrible things to the people who loved me most, and it would have done horrible things to me.

These are heavy thoughts for a young Christian to deal with, but let me save you a lot of heartache and stress by telling you what took me years to figure out: You will not meet everyone's expectations! Why do I know this? I know this because your parents are not you, your church leaders are not you, and you are not God. You will mess up one way or another. Unless your name is Jesus and you were born in Nazareth around the year 0, it is inevitable. And even Jesus didn't always meet the expectations of the people around him; he was nearly stoned after preaching in his hometown (Luke 4); his family thought he was crazy (Mark 3); and his disciples deserted him, for crying out loud!

At some point in time, your desires are going to shift away from the path where your parents and church leaders have guided you. This is a natural occurrence. It's called having your own thoughts, desires and opinions. When we are free to develop our own convictions, we have to wrestle with the Bible, with ourselves and with temptation. And if you never faced temptation, then you would be nothing more than some sort of robot Kingdom Kid Christian, which is most certainly *not* God's plan.

The inevitability of not meeting others' expectations is both good and bad. It's bad because your parents and church leaders only want what's best for you, and most of the time they are right! Sin and worldly desires aren't best for you. However, it is good because God expects you to take ownership of your soul—you and no one else.

Perfect in Getting Back Up

The message of the gospel is not about attaining perfection; Jesus has already attained perfection for us. It is about receiving grace and getting back up when we fall. Jesus' message of grace teaches us that although it is not okay to fall into sin, it is okay to get back up out of it! This holds true even for Kingdom Kids. What *is* different for Kingdom Kids is that we often feel like we are an exception. We think we're not allowed to struggle or make mistakes. We worry that because so many people have high expectations for us, our sins will have a much greater effect on people.

These feelings are valid because to an extent they are true. There are a lot of people who love us and want us to succeed spiritually, so of course it would hurt them to see us fall. But you must separate these assumptions and fears about *people* from your walk with *God*. You have to give yourself the freedom to stop obsessing over what people think, and deal with your struggles as they affect you and your relationship with God.

If you fail to do this, then everything becomes about people instead of God. In a way, these people then become your god, rather than God himself. It's not that we don't care about people and how our decisions may hurt them, but we focus *first* on God. We decide to obey him and live righteously for him and not for people.

Proverbs 24:16 says, "Though a righteous man falls seven times, he rises again, but the wicked are brought down by calamity."

This scripture helps explain this idea perfectly. It paints a picture of a man who falls down seven times, but gets back up seven times. In the Bible, the number seven symbolizes perfection. So although you may not be able to be the perfect human being who never falls, you can be perfect in getting back up from falling! The Bible teaches that we are righteous if we keep getting back up when we fall. I certainly had my tough times through high school, as you have read about already, but I am still a disciple today because I chose to get back up and reconnect with God like I did that early morning at teen camp.

Peter is a great example of getting back up when you fall. In Matthew 16, we find Jesus and his disciples discussing who people say Jesus is. Jesus directs the question to them in verse 15:

> "But what about you?" he asked. "Who do you say I am?"
>
> Simon Peter answered, "You are the Christ, the Son of the living God."
>
> Jesus replied, "Blessed are you, Simon son of Jonah, for this was not revealed to you by man, but by my Father in heaven." (Matthew 16:15–17)

Not bad so far for Peter. He answers the question correctly and is on his way to becoming one of the foremost leaders in the first-century church. On the day of my baptism, I felt very similar to the way Peter must have been feeling here. I was doing the right thing; I gave the right answers, and I was on my way to a successful spiritual life as a disciple of Christ; it was a great day and a great feeling.

But let's read on in verse 21 of the same chapter in Matthew:

> From that time on Jesus began to explain to his disciples that he must go to Jerusalem and suffer many things at the hands of the elders, chief priests and teachers of the law, and that he must be killed and on the third day be raised to life.
>
> Peter took him aside and began to rebuke him. "Never, Lord!" he said. "This shall never happen to you!"
>
> Jesus turned and said to Peter, "Get behind me, Satan! You are a stumbling block to me; you do not have in mind the things of God, but the things of men."
> (Mathew 16:21–23)

What a colossal change of events! Can a person fall any further than this? Peter just went from being told that he was blessed and had received divine revelation to being told that he was Satan! Despite Peter's earlier victory, Jesus had a lot of work to complete in order to mold Peter's character into what it needed to be for the glory of God.

I relate to Peter. Despite the magnificent day of my baptism and all the encouragement and support I received from my friends and family in the church, it didn't take long for me to forget all the convictions that I had once held so passionately. I forsook my first love and started falling into sin once more. How did I go from being baptized at a church retreat in Palm Springs to lying to my parents and going to parties with my school friends to drink? As the weeks and months passed after my baptism, my heart and convictions changed in such subtle ways that I hardly noticed the difference until it was almost too late.

Thankfully, Peter's story has a happy ending (as does mine...although of course my story isn't over!). After the death and resurrection of Jesus, Peter did amazing things to help start the Christian movement. Peter is a classic story in the Bible of a man who was perfect in getting back up, and there is no reason why you and I can't do the same!

1. How much pressure do you feel to meet the expectations of parents, Christian friends and other church members? How does it help you to know that it is God's expectations that mean the most?

2. Write down how the following statement hits you: "The message of the gospel is not about attaining perfection; Jesus has already attained perfection for us. It is about receiving grace and getting back up when we fall."

3. In what ways can you relate to Peter and his spiritual highs and lows?

KEEPING IT REAL
'I'm Not Allowed to Have Fun?!'

It was a few weeks after my senior year in high school. A group of my friends from church—guys and girls, all disciples—wanted to go on a five-hundred-mile road trip to San Francisco. We were a week away from hitting the road when my parents caught wind of my trip plans...and within twenty-four hours, the trip was canceled. My parents had talked to other leaders and to some of the people who were going on the trip, and all of a sudden nobody wanted to go anymore. I was totally surprised, but more than that, I was furious! My friends and I were supposed to have a wonderful road trip to San Francisco! What happened?

The same day that I discovered what my parents had done, I got a call from my mom saying that they wanted to talk to me about the trip I had been planning. So I came home and the battle began.

"Why did you have to go and ruin our road trip? What could you possibly think would go wrong?" I asked.

My mom said, "Drew, you don't realize how easy it is for things to go wrong, especially when girls and guys are together. Your safety and even your purity could be at stake on a trip like this."

"Purity? What are you talking about? We weren't going out there to sin! We were going out there to enjoy a fun trip with our friends. That's all!"

"We understand that, but the fact is that without older, more spiritual people going with you guys on this trip, we don't think it's a good idea."

"So I'm not allowed to have fun?"

"Of course you are! But if your 'fun' doesn't glorify God...then no."

Of course, going into the feud, I had already known I had no chance of convincing my parents to let me go on the trip. Besides, all of my friends who were supposed to go on the trip had begun feeling like it was a bad idea, and even if they didn't feel that way, they were still too scared to go against the wishes of their parents and our church leaders.

I was so angry. I remember thinking, "I'm never going to be able to do anything without my parents and other Christians telling me what to do." My parents didn't trust that I could stay out of trouble or that the guys and girls could stay pure, so the entire thing was canceled. Even though I had repented of going to parties, even though I had reconnected with God at camp, even though I had graduated from high school as a faithful disciple, I *still* felt trapped.

Respecting Your Parents' and Leaders' Decisions

I have had many experiences like the incident of The Road Trip That Wasn't. Conflicts like this have continued to happen even after high school and throughout college. There have been numerous times when I've felt like my parents and church leaders were taking away all my chances to live a free life.

Maybe this hasn't happened to you yet, but the fact is, if you are a member of a biological family or of God's church family for any length of time, you will eventually disagree with your parents or with your spiritual leaders about something. When you feel like your parents are making decisions without really considering your feelings, you don't have to like it, and you don't even have to agree with it, but I do believe it makes your life a zillion times easier if you at least try to understand where your parents are coming from.

I did a horrible job of trying to understand when my parents dismantled my road trip to San Francisco. Instead of taking the time to realize that they were only trying to protect us, I reacted emotionally. Sure I didn't agree with their decision, but that didn't make my reactions right. It is *not* okay to be disrespectful, arrogant or sarcastic with our parents (as I am sorry to say I have done so many times in my life). Reacting sinfully and immaturely only makes it worse for both you and your parents.

Obey Your Parents

Remember this scripture?

> Children, obey your parents in the Lord, for this is right. "Honor your father and mother"—which is the first commandment with a promise—"that it may go well with you and that you may enjoy long life on the earth." (Ephesians 6:1–3)

This was my parents' favorite scripture to share with me when I was growing up. They might have even read it to my mom's stomach when I was still in the womb! I knew it very well from reading it at home and at Sunday school. Though it is certainly one of those scriptures that Kingdom Kids can quote in their sleep, there is a reason we know it so well: because it's the truth. There will always be authorities in our lives, and the sooner we learn to respect them, the sooner life becomes easier for us. Trust me.

Now this scripture isn't saying, "Follow your parents' every whim no matter the circumstance until the end of time." This scripture is speaking to children. I don't know what God's cutoff is for when children become adults, but I would assume that as long as you are still a teenager living under your parents' roof and reliant on their support to get through life, this verse applies to you. As much as it may frustrate us sometimes, I can attest to the fact that obeying your parents' wishes early on in life is favored by God (and makes your life better). I have a large number of Time Outs, spankings, groundings, car accidents and other wonderful achievements on my résumé to prove it. As children and teens, we are called by God to obey our parents.

Yes, this is how it should be, and no, you won't be a child for the rest of your life.

Honoring Our Parents

We are also called to honor our parents, and I believe that this rule applies beyond childhood and into adulthood. To honor our parents is to show by our hearts, words and actions that we love and respect them. As you go through your teen years and beyond, your relationship with your parents will change a lot, but it brings glory to God when you continue to honor the parents he gave you. When you are an adult, you won't be expected to obey them the way you did when you were a child, and this is part of growing up, but should we not continue to honor the two people who give so much to us throughout our lives?

I believe a great way to honor our parents, especially in situations when we disagree with them or feel pressured to be someone we don't want to be, is to make the effort to first understand where they are coming from (as I mentioned before), and to keep in mind that they are acting out of love for us.

The truth is that our parents and church leaders love us very much. They want us to be safe and successful in our spiritual walk. You may not feel like they do sometimes (and it is normal for sons and daughters to feel like this every once in a while), but they do, and it is vital that you understand this. It's hard to be angry at people who you know are doing their best to love you, protect you and take care of you.

I've given my parents way more than their fair share of grief over the years, and I am so thankful that they have never given up on me, even during my most rebellious, deceitful times. I'm grateful for the faith they have imparted to me and my brother from birth, for the closeness we have enjoyed over the years, and for their willingness to take me on when I was being head-strong and foolish.

In this book I have shared a lot of the conflicts my parents and I had during my teen years—somehow the many happy conversations we had don't make for such fun illustrations—but now I am thankful for the times when we disagreed. Those conflicts tested and refined my faith and our relationship, and in the end, they have brought us closer together. To this day I am very close to my parents, and I owe them everything.

Church Leaders

I have not always been a great example of the humility and co-operative spirit God calls us to have in following church leaders. As you know, throughout most of my teen and campus life as a Christian, I failed to follow my spiritual leaders the way God has called me to. God has put great people in my life through the years, but I sometimes gave those people a hard time when I didn't understand or agree with their advice. However, having said that, this probably makes me the perfect person to tell you about all of the unnecessary hardship you will experience if you don't learn to follow and honor your leaders in a way that glorifies God!

Let's take a look at someone else who had trouble respecting a godly leader and following simple instructions:

> Now Naaman was commander of the army of the king of Aram. He was a great man in the sight of his master and highly regarded, because through him the LORD had given victory to Aram. He was a valiant soldier, but he had leprosy....
> So Naaman went with his horses and chariots and stopped at the door of Elisha's house. Elisha sent a messenger to say to him, "Go, wash yourself seven times in the Jordan,

and your flesh will be restored and you will be cleansed."

But Naaman went away angry and said, "I thought that he would surely come out to me and stand and call on the name of the LORD his God, wave his hand over the spot and cure me of my leprosy. Are not Abana and Pharpar, the rivers of Damascus, better than any of the waters of Israel? Couldn't I wash in them and be cleansed?" So he turned and went off in a rage.

Naaman's servants went to him and said, "My father, if the prophet had told you to do some great thing, would you not have done it? How much more, then, when he tells you, 'Wash and be cleansed'!" So he went down and dipped himself in the Jordan seven times, as the man of God had told him, and his flesh was restored and became clean like that of a young boy. (2 Kings 5:1, 9–14)

Here we see Naaman, a man with leprosy searching for a way to be cured. The good thing is that at least Naaman knows that he has leprosy and needs help. Sadly, many of us Kingdom Kids have issues in our character or lifestyle, but we are too self-right-eous or oblivious to even notice!

When Naaman is instructed by a prophet to go and wash in a river to be cleansed of leprosy, he immediately dismisses the advice as rubbish. It isn't until his own servants reason with him that Naaman decides to at least try what Elisha has suggested. Interestingly, our leaders at church often suggest things to us that sound far more reasonable than dunking yourself seven times in muddy water, and yet we still refuse to follow their advice.

I do not think that it would have been wrong for Naaman to respectfully ask Elisha, "I understand what you are telling me to do, but I just don't see the logic behind it. Can you please help me see what you see here, Elisha, so that I may have the faith that you have?"

But instead of reacting this way, Naaman bolts off in anger, rejecting the prophet's advice. Likewise, when we are put in a situation where our teen leaders ask us to do something—maybe it's something simple, like being more giving at church; or something more challenging, like changing an aspect of our character; or something really difficult, like not dating a certain person at school—there is nothing wrong with respectfully asking questions.

Sometimes Kingdom Kids think they have to just blindly obey everything their parents and leaders say without speaking up or asking questions. But that's not true! It is fine to ask people why they are giving us the advice they're giving. It's fine to tell them you don't understand and to discuss the things you disagree with. Otherwise, you'll end up with a bad attitude! It's *not* fine to obey grudgingly or angrily, or to harbor resentment in your heart. Asking questions and having honest discussions is good and right and healthy, and I bet you'll learn a lot in the process.

Importance of Humility

It is clear that God only wanted to bless Naaman, but it took an act of humility in order for the blessing to take place. Why would we be any different? God was trying to cure Naaman of leprosy. He was looking out for Naaman's best interests, but all Naaman could see was the way that God expected it to be done.

Sometimes (okay maybe a lot of times) we have our own idea of how we think leaders should lead us. And then if they don't do things our way, we get mad or sulky. But think about this: If leaders always did everything the way *we* think they should, *they* wouldn't be the leaders, would they?

I know it can be hard to find humility when you really disagree with what your parents or spiritual leaders think. Some of the things that may be running through your mind when you don't agree with your leaders might be similar to things that I have felt:

- The "advice" that I keep getting feels more like orders than actual advice. I feel like I am being controlled.
- What if I really disagree with what my church leaders think I should do?
- It doesn't seem fair that I am all of a sudden labeled as a prideful person just because I disagree.

Sound familiar? I've felt all of these things at times. But as I grow older, I'm starting to see some things differently.

Now let's be clear: Some biblical matters are non-debatable no-no's, and we have zero business trying to argue about them. But then there are opinion matters—things that aren't sin—and people will have different opinions about what's okay and what's not okay. In these areas of life, it is fine for us to have differing opinions with other people, but it is not okay to start living like our opinion is the only one that is important.

Did I have valid feelings and opinions about what I thought was best, back in high school and in college? Of course! But I also think that for many years I was missing the point. *The thing we must realize is that God loves humility far more than he loves the best-sounding opinions.* So many times, I just wanted to prove my point, when God was more concerned about my heart.

Church leaders (and parents) are put in our lives to help us and guide us in our spiritual walk. And it is especially in these types of relationships that God calls us to be humble. Like Naaman, I needed to first humble myself before I could even *hear* the advice people were trying to give me...and most of the time, that advice was going to protect me or even save my spiritual life in some way.

You can't talk things out rationally if you are being prideful. You can't hear if you don't listen! And in the end, remember that you have *a relationship* with your parents and your leaders. It's not about just following advice; it's about having a relationship. They don't want to just boss you around—they want to know what you really think and feel. They want to help you grow. Your thoughts and feelings may not change their advice...but even then, they are not your enemy.

Parents and leaders are humans too, and so they understand the struggles that we are going through. When we forget that, when we turn a conversation into a battle of opposite opinions, we hurt the spiritual relationship that we could have—that God wants us to have.

Humility in these situations doesn't mean to just give up your opinion and do everything your leaders say. It has more to do with being open-minded and understanding a different point of view. I used to only see how I thought *my* opinion was right and made sense to *me* and was best for *me*, but I didn't realize that it might not have been the best for other people around me. The Road Trip That Wasn't is the perfect example of this. To me, the trip was a great idea! It all made perfect sense. I wasn't trying to do anything wrong or commit a whole bunch of sin.

From my point of view, the trip wasn't bad, and I had reasons for why I thought it was going to be a *good* thing...but what I refused to see was how my trip might have affected others besides me. I lacked the maturity to consider whether it was the best idea for a whole group.

Helpful Feedback

Now this may surprise you (or maybe not), but because Kingdom Kids have been part of the church for a while, your observations and opinions can actually be helpful to your church leaders. If you are able to offer your thoughts with a mature attitude—remembering that your own happiness and opinions aren't the only things that matter—your ideas, suggestions and criticisms can be useful.

The truth is that our leaders, just like our parents, love us and want us to do well. They advise us the way they do because they want to help our relationship with God. We still have to decide whether or not to follow their advice, but when we choose to open ourselves up and to value humility and a real relationship more than our own wonderful-sounding opinions, we can begin to see things from God's point of view...and maybe even from our leaders' point of view!

Leaders Are Not Perfect

It is important for us to remember that no leader is perfect, even if they are really trying to do what is right. And every once in a while you could even have a leader who does not have the right motives, who is acting out of pride, and who does not have your best interests in mind. I have known people who have experienced this, and there have been times when I have experienced this myself. My observation is that if this is the true character of a leader, God will deal with them accordingly, and others will see their problems and bring them to correction (and ultimately ask them to step out of leadership if it gets to that point).

But even if this is the case for you, your humility in expressing your concerns to your parents and other leaders will be needed and appreciated. Then you must trust that God will work with all who are concerned to help them grow and change.

Finding Freedom

As I have grown in my humility over the years (and I'm still growing), I have been amazed by the *freedom* I have found in my relationships with my parents and with the leaders God has put in my life. I no longer feel trapped when people give me advice—I feel grateful that they care enough to want to help me. I no longer feel pressure to perform and do whatever they say; I feel free to have real relationships and real discussions, and now I feel free from the *pride* that kept me bound to my own opinions!

The Bible says, "God opposes the proud but gives grace to the humble" (James 4:6), and I hope that you too can feel set free by God's grace.

GET REAL

1. In what ways can you relate to what I felt about my parents canceling my trip to San Francisco?
2. When you have been in situations where you didn't get your own way in discussions with your parents, how have you responded? Why is it helpful for you to consider what your parents might be thinking?
3. When you read the story of Naaman, what do you learn about following constructive advice?
4. Is there any helpful feedback you want to give to your leaders? Why will sharing this with humility help them to hear you?

KEEPING IT REAL
'I'm Not Feeling It'

It was my freshman year in college, and I was at a campus ministry retreat, but I just wasn't "feeling it" like everyone else. I was uninspired and unenthusiastic, while everyone else seemed totally excited to be there. It was obvious that I wasn't into it, because I wasn't going around saying things like "This is so awesome!" or "I'm so encouraged to be here!" or any of the other spiritual catchphrases and buzzwords that everyone else was saying.

Over time, I guess these types of events had become predictable and uninteresting for me. Sometimes I felt the same way about church services and devotionals; I'm sorry to say that even my relationships with other disciples had started to feel bland and boring. I got tired of having the same conversations at church and at retreats or camps. I wasn't getting much out of the sermons I heard—it seemed like I had heard it all before. It had been a long time since I felt inspired.

The truth was that I had become lazy and unwilling to connect with people in different ways than I was used to. I had lost my spiritual edge once again in my life and was faced with the need to repent.

It actually wasn't until much later, after that campus retreat (and a number of others), that I realized that this feeling of boredom and lack of inspiration was coming from my pride. Since I had already experienced these types of retreats and other experiences so many times before, I had felt that I was better or above the experience in some way, and so I was unwilling to be moved spiritually or emotionally. I wasn't above anything; the reality was that my pride was actually bringing me lower because it was keeping me from growing any more in my walk with God.

Been There, Done That

I have been a Kingdom Kid since I was in the womb. My parents were already devout Christians before I was even born. Going to church and being around Christianity has been a part of my life as long as I can remember. After going to church for a while, disciples can tend to pick up a certain kind of "been there, done that" attitude toward the Christian life that greatly hinders any further spiritual growth in that person's life. The scary thing is that for Kingdom Kids, this attitude can be developed even before we begin to study the Bible to become a Christian!

In the previous chapter, we discussed the importance of humility in our spiritual walk. I can tell you from personal experience that the minute you begin to lean on your own habits and understanding is the minute you stop growing as a person and as a disciple. If you stop searching outside of what you already know, how will you ever learn new things? And if you aren't learning new things, how do you expect to grow?

Proverbs 14:12 says, "There is a way that seems right to a man, but in the end it leads to death." Even Socrates, probably the most famous philosopher of all time, said, "As for me, all I know is that I know nothing." Growth begins with humility. We must become humble if we want to learn, and especially if we want to live like Jesus.

As a Kingdom Kid, you may have spent your whole life learning about God, but that doesn't mean you know everything! We all have a lifetime of learning ahead of us.

Know-It-Alls

Kingdom Kids can feel that they know just about all of the answers, and in some ways, they sort of do! Most of us can come up with a good, righteous-sounding, teen-leader-impressing, parent-pleasing answer to any spiritual question that is thrown our way. We can do this because we know what is expected. After sitting through countless sermons, devotionals and quiet times, it is safe to say we have heard all of the spiritual jargon that is out there.

In other words, we know how to speak "Bible." We also know how our church operates. We know what people do when they think someone is struggling spiritually. We know how to react when someone asks us why we weren't at church or why we aren't engaged in the fellowship. But just because you know what a spiritual person *should* be saying does not mean you know the *right* thing to say.

Just to clarify, the right thing to say is always the truth. To give you an example, my early Bible studies went something like this...

After reading a scripture about how God blesses humility:

Teen leader: "So, Drew, what do you think about the scripture we just read?"

Me: "Well, I think it's saying we need to be more humble and love God."

Teen leader: "Okay. But how do you feel about that? How is this going in your life?"

Me: "Well, I think I need to try to be more humble and love God more because that is what he wants me to do."

Teen leader: "Argh! I didn't ask you to regurgitate what we just read. I asked what it means to *you,* Drew!"

Me: "It means that, for me, I need to try to be more humble—you know, not prideful—and love God. And stuff."

Teen leader: "Helloooooooooo!!! Earth to Drew! Do you actually agree with this scripture? Is this hard for you to follow? When was the last time you struggled with showing humility?! Do you feel anything about the Bible at all?" (This isn't how my teen leaders actually talked to me, but I was so difficult to deal with that I bet this is how they *wanted* to respond at times.)

True Talk, Not Drew Talk

I knew that the Scriptures called me to respond a certain way; I also knew the kind of answers my teen leaders were looking for. Or at least I thought I did. The reality was that I didn't know the right answers at all! The "right" answers I gave were usually not what my teen ministry leaders were looking for; what they wanted was the *truth.* They wanted to see my *heart.*

I spent a lot of time as a Kingdom Kid giving spiritual-sounding answers just to seem godly and to keep teen leaders and other people from knowing what was really going on, either because I didn't want to be honest or because I knew that they would disagree with the way I was doing things. Sadly, the only person that I ever fooled by doing all of this was myself.

Absolute and Abstract

There are two sides of the brain: the *absolute* and the *abstract*. Kingdom Kids grow up learning all the absolutes of the Bible (we learn it practically by osmosis), all of the dos and don'ts, all of the "right" and "wrong" ways to respond to the Scriptures. But all of this only covers half of who we are and what God wants from us. Although we are lucky to have "the rules" figured out already, we still need to figure out the rest.

God doesn't just want our obedience; he wants our affection. It is our duty to look deeper than the simple answers of *yes* and *no* that we learned as kids, and work to find the substance of our own unique heart and soul. A good example of this is the rich young man in the book of Mark:

> As Jesus started on his way, a man ran up to him and fell on his knees before him. "Good teacher," he asked, "what must I do to inherit eternal life?"
>
> "Why do you call me good?" Jesus answered. "No one is good—except God alone. You know the commandments: 'Do not murder, do not commit adultery, do not steal, do not give false testimony, do not defraud, honor your father and mother.'"
>
> "Teacher," he declared, "all these I have kept since I was a boy."
>
> Jesus looked at him and loved him. "One thing you lack," he said. "Go, sell everything you have and give to the poor, and you will have treasure in heaven. Then come, follow me."
>
> At this the man's face fell. He went away sad, because he had great wealth. (Mark 10:17–22)

Here is a man who knows all of the absolutes. He's like a first-century, Jewish version of a Kingdom Kid: He knows the commandments and has followed them faithfully his whole life.

Certainly this is a guy who has some things figured out. He is already light years ahead of others who haven't even heard of the commandments of God, and he has only just met Jesus! But when Jesus decides to bring the issue into the deeper waters of the young man's heart, the guy is stopped dead in his tracks.

It is at this point that all the understanding and knowledge we've received as Kingdom Kids is thrown out the window. Because on this issue—the question of our *heart*—all human beings stand on an even playing field, no matter how much we know. The question then becomes this: Are you willing to give up the things that keep you from loving God? (Remember that wealth, popularity, girlfriends and boyfriends do not go with you to heaven.) The right answer to this question is yes, and of course you know that, but is this really something you are willing to say yes to? Your actions throughout the course of your life will reveal the answer to that question, not your answers in a Bible study.

It's All About Me

According to www.dictionary.com, the word *entitlement* means "the right to guaranteed benefits."

Going to a great church offers a number of benefits that are so often taken for granted by Christians, especially Kingdom Kids. Among countless other blessings, we get a great support system of family and friends who love us; free help in our efforts to get to heaven; a full social life with lots of fun, fulfilling things to do; free guidance counseling; networking for jobs...I could go on and on! The thing about all of this is that we are not entitled to any of it. The only reason we have all of this is because Jesus died and rose again, and people have chosen to believe that he is Lord.

Unfortunately, because we have grown up in this culture, we just assume that we deserve it, or even worse, we totally lose sight of its positive impact on our lives. Being grateful for what we have as disciples of Jesus inspires us to maintain a modest, open attitude toward the church, an attitude that is crucial if we are going to grow as Christians.

Because of our familiarity with the church system and culture, we Kingdom Kids can acquire a sense of entitlement. We think we deserve the blessings of God because we've always had them and we have never known life without them. It's kind of like growing up in a rich country like America. We expect to always have electricity, and we get mad if the power goes out for a long time...but now that I live in Cambodia, I don't think that way. Power shortages happen a lot here, but no one complains. They are just happy to have electricity because a lot of people here have never had it!

An attitude of entitlement builds up the wall around our hearts even more, and keeps us from growing. When this happens, we lose one of the most significant aspects of what it means to be part of a Christian fellowship: gratitude.

Entitlement—Nothing New

As Kingdom Kids, whether we choose to give our lives to God or not, we can all agree that we have been amazingly blessed. We could have been raised in horrible living situations, but instead, God allowed us to be raised in godly families and in a church full of love. Some people never experience those things. Sadly, many of us Kingdom Kids just don't appreciate the blessings we have been given.

Not surprisingly, this is not the first time that God has had to deal with this kind of attitude:

He guided them with the cloud by day
    and with light from the fire all night.
He split the rocks in the desert
    and gave them water as abundant as the seas;
he brought streams out of a rocky crag
    and made water flow down like rivers.
But they continued to sin against him,
    rebelling in the desert against the Most High.
They willfully put God to the test
    by demanding the food they craved.
They spoke against God, saying,
    "Can God spread a table in the desert?
When he struck the rock, water gushed out,
    and streams flowed abundantly.
But can he also give us food?
    Can he supply meat for his people?"
When the LORD heard them, he was very angry;
    his fire broke out against Jacob,
    and his wrath rose against Israel,
for they did not believe in God
    or trust in his deliverance.
Yet he gave a command to the skies above
    and opened the doors of the heavens;
he rained down manna for the people to eat,
    he gave them the grain of heaven.
Men ate the bread of angels;
    he sent them all the food they could eat.
He let loose the east wind from the heavens
    and led forth the south wind by his power.
He rained meat down on them like dust,
    flying birds like sand on the seashore.
He made them come down inside their camp,
    all around their tents.
They ate till they had more than enough,
    for he had given them what they craved.
But before they turned from the food they craved,

> even while it was still in their mouths,
> God's anger rose against them;
> > he put to death the sturdiest among them,
> > cutting down the young men of Israel.
> In spite of all this, they kept on sinning;
> > in spite of his wonders, they did not believe.
> (Psalm 78:14–32)

The Israelites obviously had some essential concepts about God extremely confused. This psalm paints a pretty bad picture of their hearts. They wanted a whole lot from God and got fed up with him when they didn't get what they wanted. They were chasing one fulfillment after another and developed a sense of entitlement for the blessings that God had given them.

First they wanted to be freed from the Egyptians; then they wanted to go to the promised land; then they wanted water and food; then they wanted *more* water and *better* food, and so on and so on and so on. The humbling thing is that the story of the Israelites can apply to many Kingdom Kids, especially me.

If Psalm 78 were written about me instead of the Israelites it would probably go something like this:

Psalm 78: Ode to Drew

> He guided Drew into the most loving of homes,
> > and gave him parents who showed him the truth of God.
> He saved him from the hand of Satan
> > and fed him with the deepest love.
> He brought youth ministers to look after him
> > and made friendships easy for him to find.
> But Drew continued to sin against him,
> > rebelling at home and at school.
> He willfully put God to the test
> > by demanding the satisfaction that he craved.
> He spoke against God, saying,

"I am not free, these people keep me from living the way
that I want!"
When God forgave his sins and offered him hope,
Drew asked, "But can you not also make me amazingly
successful and important?
Can you supply me with popularity at school, and with a
girlfriend?"
When the LORD heard him he was angry.
Cutting down Drew's pride, he willed his parents to discover his sin,
and they grounded him his entire junior year in high
school...

...and I could go on for another 500 verses.

Although it is not in any way righteous, it is at least understandable that Kingdom Kids can grow up with a sense of entitlement
to all the wonderful benefits of the church. But as we mature
in our understanding of life and the world, we should have a
better sense of just how blessed we are. We don't *deserve* the
great family, church or lives we have; God doesn't *owe* us any
blessings. We shouldn't feel entitled to the blessings we receive
as disciples, we should feel grateful.

No matter how much I messed up, the people at church were
always there to love me and take care of me. My youth ministers
took countless hours out of their schedules to spend time with
me and help me deal with issues at home or at school. The lack
of gratitude that I often displayed for these blessings did not
please God. And my ingratitude set me up for a fall spiritually.
The scary thing is, if our hearts do not become humble and
grateful, we are in danger of slowly drifting further and further
away from God and from our relationships in the church, and
then the benefits we've taken for granted will disappear.

We need to take Philippians 4:12 to heart:

> I know what it is to be in need, and I know what it is to have plenty. I have learned the secret of being content in any and every situation, whether well fed or hungry, whether living in plenty or in want.

My belief is that the secret Paul is describing here is gratitude—namely, gratitude for what Jesus did for him on the cross. When we stop focusing on all that we do not have and instead consider the glorious inheritance that we *do* have as disciples of Christ, we can find contentment no matter what.

As Kingdom Kids, we understand what it means to have plenty and to be well fed. We have been blessed with far more love than the average teenager has experienced. Kingdom Kids actually have more cause to feel content than Paul did! How dare we continue to live our Christian lives with an attitude of entitlement toward the church. We should be thanking people at church all of the time for what they have done for us.

Most importantly, we need to remember the cross. That is our greatest blessing and the source of all our other blessings in our lives. When we appreciate what Jesus did on the cross, we realize how rich we are and how much we don't deserve the life God has given us. We understand that the life of a Christian is the most wonderful life of freedom there is.

Pride Goes Before the Fall

Pride is the Kingdom Kid's archenemy. We all deal with it in countless ways that hurt our own hearts and hurt other people too. When we first make the decision to become disciples, most of us adopt a humble attitude toward the Scriptures and our ministry leaders. However, over time, this humility has the tendency to slip away.

Kingdom Kids can sometimes have a difficult time relating to non-Kingdom Kids in a meaningful way. We also tend to be more critical of our church and youth or campus ministry. This is an unfortunate reality in many youth and campus ministries, and it leads to divisions in the church.

Baptized teens tend to see themselves as different from—and at times even better than—other teens in the church who have not yet decided to give their lives to Christ. This can lead to cliques in teen ministries. You might be thinking, "But wait! There can't be cliques in the church!" Well, there *shouldn't* be cliques in the church, and of course the Bible speaks against cliques, or factions, in the fellowship—and yet we are all sinful, and so we have to work hard to keep unity in the church and in our ministries.

In my teen ministry there was always an extreme disconnect between the teens who were baptized or studying the Bible and those who weren't. Many of us had gone through Sunday school together as toddlers and as elementary school students. However, as we got older and some of us became disciples, we divided into two unofficial groups: the Christians and the non-Christians.

Certainly, those of us who became disciples did have some important things in common, and those brought us closer, but it wasn't right when we looked down on the teens who hadn't yet become Christians. It wasn't right when we banded together in a "holier than thou" group, or when we left people out, or when we made the other teens feel like they didn't belong in our ministry anymore. Sadly, we didn't even realize we were doing anything wrong.

I find this to be a very dangerous (and common) scenario for the community of Kingdom Kids in a congregation—and very contradictory to how Jesus taught his disciples to act. Looking back on it all, I wish I had spent more time building friendships with the Kingdom Kids who had not made the decision to become disciples. Whether it would have changed their decision or not, it would have at least made them feel more welcome. It would have also helped them to see that Kingdom Kid disciples really were committed to humbling themselves like Jesus.

The Spiritually Initiated

Another pride problem that plagues many Kingdom Kids is our familiarity with the church "system." I don't mean to imply that the church has some rigid formula of how it does things, but we all understand the way things work in our church: what people expect, what's normal, how disciples should talk and act. We can do and say all the right things on the outside and never look like we need help spiritually.

As Kingdom Kids who have recently become disciples, even though we are "baby Christians," we can begin to feel like we are above the expectations that "regular" disciples follow because we have been around the fellowship for so long. Sure, it's good for disciples to practice daily prayer and Bible study; sure, disciples need close friends in the church who can help them grow spiritually—but *we* don't really need those things as much. We may not say it, or even consciously think it, but sometimes we make ourselves an exception.

We think, "I've been reading the Bible my whole life; it doesn't matter if I skip my times with God whenever I feel like it." Or we tell ourselves, "I don't really need to talk to anyone about how I'm doing spiritually; I already know what they're going to say." Even if we don't *admit* these things, we *act* that way. Our actions tell other people, "I don't have to do the normal disciple stuff; I've got this disciple thing down all by myself. I don't need to get close to any new people; we are far too different and won't understand each other."

We slowly fall into our own habits and our own way of doing things, and because no one has corrected us about it before, or maybe because we've slipped so slowly that no one has noticed, we grow confident that our way is the right way.

Pride: Subtle or Spewing

Some people's pride and arrogance spew out of their pores like hot lava from a volcano. This describes me perfectly...and maybe some of you other Kingdom Kids as well. But many other people have a more subtle pride, a quiet pride. Quiet pride is dangerous because, since no one notices it, the person can slip away into their own world without being bothered; loud pride (like mine) is dangerous because our outward confidence might pull others down with us or push people away.

I must once again confess by saying that I have been prideful more often than I can remember. I have separated myself time and again from people because I thought I couldn't relate to them, and only once they had somehow proven their ability to relate to me did I open myself up to being their friend. I have put up a front of spirituality that even my closest friends were unable to see through. This is not the attitude of Jesus, and I wish I'd been different.

You've heard it said, "Don't learn the hard way." I learned these things the hard way, and I'm sharing them with you so you can do things differently during your teen years.

We have been blessed in a profound way, and now we have the opportunity to spread the love that has been shown to us our entire lives. Let us realize our potential, and become the disciples Jesus has taught us to be.

Staying Inspired

I once read a book about church movements throughout history, and I realized a stunning similarity between a lot of movements and my own spiritual walk. Usually, church movements experience a time of extreme growth and spiritual revival, and then after hitting a peak, the growth stops, and the movement begins to fall. At this point, the movement either disappears, or in order to save itself, it becomes a steady institution and no longer enjoys the growth it once experienced.

Sadly, I realized that my own spiritual walk was very similar to these Christian movements. After many years of being part of the church and being baptized as a young teen and learning many great things, I had finally reached a peak and was no longer willing to be inspired and grow. I didn't sustain the growth I'd enjoyed in my early years as a disciple, and I started to falter spiritually. But instead of disappearing and leaving the church, I went into a sort of spiritual survival mode where I wasn't growing, but I wasn't going to fall away either—I just *was*.

The interesting thing about the similarities between church movements and my own personal spirituality is that they show that what is true for the individuals in a church is also true for the church as a whole. If we as Kingdom Kids don't stay committed to learning new things and growing, the church will likely do the same because we make up a large population of the church!

Now, it is understandable if you are not totally inspired every time you hear a Sunday sermon. And it is okay if every retreat and teen camp doesn't make you feel amazing inside (as I shared at the beginning of this chapter). This is actually normal, and means that you have to work harder to find inspiration in your life. It is okay if things don't inspire you sometimes, but it isn't okay to give up and just never be inspired at all.

Some things that have helped me to find inspiration in my life outside of normal church gatherings are

- Studying books written about the Bible that go into depth about what the Scriptures mean and how they apply to my life.
- Reading biographies of influential Christians throughout history.
- Building relationships with people who are inspired.
- Striving to continue to learn new things about God.
- While at Sunday services, camps or retreats, trying to connect with people you haven't connected to in the past and in different ways than you are used to connecting.

These are just some things that help me, but I am sure you can find many other ways to keep yourself inspired and alive. It is essential that we continue to grow as Christians. Jesus himself was already perfect when he came down to the earth, and yet he could still be amazed by people's faith (Luke 7:9), and he still found it necessary to go to God in prayer and to visit the temple to hear the word of God spoken. None of us is anywhere near as righteous as Jesus, and so of course we must continue to fight to remain inspired and live impactful lives for God!

What Jesus says in Revelation 2:3–4 calls us all higher:

> "You have persevered and have endured hardships for my name, and have not grown weary. Yet I hold this against you: You have forsaken your first love. Remember the height from which you have fallen! Repent and do the things you did at first."

Let's all fight to stay inspired and keep our "first love" for Christ!

GET REAL

1. Explain how the rich young man who came to Jesus is much like someone who has grown up in the church.

2. What similarities do you see between the real Psalm 78 and the "Ode to Drew" version? In what ways do you relate to my rewriting of the psalm?

3. At one point when I was not doing well spiritually, this is how I coped: "I went into a sort of spiritual survival mode where I wasn't growing, but I wasn't going to fall away either—I just *was*." In what ways can you relate to this?

4. What are some ways you can continue to be inspired and to inspire others?

KEEPING IT REAL
Whose Faith Am I Sharing?

I was sitting at Chili's restaurant getting time with Frank, my teen minister, eating my cheeseburger and fries and enjoying life. Frank and I always went to Chili's to talk and just hang out, and I always looked forward to it. Usually when it came to spiritual stuff, we would just talk about what I was reading and learning, and I would give short answers that were deep enough to sound like my heart was in the right place, but shallow enough that they didn't lead to anything too serious or challenging.

This time, however, Frank navigated right through the smokescreen.

"So, what have you been reading in the Bible lately?" Frank asked.

"Proverbs," I said.

"I am pretty sure you were reading Proverbs last time we hung out," said Frank, with his eyebrows raised.

"Oh, right. Well, there is plenty in there to learn I guess."

Frank's tone got serious. "Actually, I think you tell me Psalms or Proverbs ninety percent of the time that I ask you what you are reading. Do you actually enjoy these books, or are they just the first thing that comes to your mind when I ask you that question?"

"Uhhh…Yes." (What else was I supposed to say? I couldn't lie! And I did enjoy Psalms and Proverbs. I was sort of reading them at all times. Frank saw right through me, as he had done on several occasions in my life.)

"Yes, you enjoy reading Psalms and Proverbs, or yes, you can't think of anything else?"

"Uhhh..." (As you can see, the word *uhhh* is Greek for "You just busted me and I have nothing to say.")

As our lunch continued, it became obvious how weak my faith had become. Frank and I shared our faith with the waitress—actually, that's not true. Frank shared his faith with her; I sat there with my mouth hanging open and my brain empty of thoughts. When the waitress asked me the name of our church, I totally blanked! "Uhhh...I don't have a card. Frank do you have a card on you?"

"Sure I do," said Frank, stepping in to save me. "We go to a great church in the area, and it would be great if you could come by..."

In that moment, I realized that I hadn't been feeding myself spiritually with meaningful Bible study, and so I had no faith to share. When Frank dropped me off at home, I had a lot to think about.

Why was I so afraid to invite someone to church?

Why did I always say I was reading Proverbs?

Did I need someone to tell me to read the Bible and share my faith?

Why couldn't I do these things on my own?

Whose faith was I sharing, Frank's or mine?

Impacting the World Around You

As you might have gathered, I had a lot of growing to do in owning my faith and sharing it with people around me. The truth is that Kingdom Kids, despite some of our shortcomings, are greatly equipped to impact the world around us, but we first need to take ownership of our faith. We need to develop our own desire to reach people so that we are sharing *our* faith instead of our parents' or teen ministers' faith. I appreciated Frank challenging me and pushing me out of my comfort zone. If it wasn't for him, I might never have awakened to the fact that I needed to develop my own passion for the world around me.

Jesus had a love for lost souls that was so deep and so passionate that no one could stop him. Forget people trying to convince him to share his faith—people tried to convince him to *stop* sharing his faith, but he wouldn't. He couldn't!

Why We Do What We Do

As we have already discussed, it is important to focus on *being* rather than *doing*. Just *doing* can lead to us going through the motions and having the wrong heart. This was my problem at Chili's, and Frank called me on it. Had I remembered that Jesus calls me to be the salt of the earth and the light of the world, maybe sharing with our waitress would have come more naturally to me.

It's easy to get sidetracked from having world impact when our Christian life keeps us so busy. We can get so caught up in our "Christian Checklist" that we forget why we do what we do and forget about our mission! Whether we are reading our Bible, praying or sharing our faith, we have to guard against doing the actions for the sake of doing them. These actions should be a part of who we are. I know I have already talked about this, but I also know that I often have to hear things several times to really get the point!

This scripture has always challenged me to the core and helped me to think about where my heart is:

> "When the Son of Man comes in his glory, and all the angels with him, he will sit on his throne in heavenly glory. All the nations will be gathered before him, and he will separate the people one from another as a shepherd separates the sheep from the goats. He will put the sheep on his right and the goats on his left.
>
> "Then the King will say to those on his right, 'Come, you who are blessed by my Father; take your inheritance, the kingdom prepared for you since the creation of the world. For I was hungry and you gave me something to eat, I was thirsty and you gave me something to drink, I was a stranger and you invited me in, I needed clothes and you clothed me, I was sick and you looked after me, I was in prison and you came to visit me.'
>
> "Then the righteous will answer him, 'Lord, when did we see you hungry and feed you, or thirsty and give you something to drink? When did we see you a stranger and invite

you in, or needing clothes and clothe you? When did we see you sick or in prison and go to visit you?'

"The King will reply, 'I tell you the truth, whatever you did for one of the least of these brothers of mine, you did for me.'" (Matthew 25:31–40)

This passage is an amazing testament to the expectations that God has for us. World impact starts with love for God. People want to know how to serve God, and the reply is: "If you want to serve me, serve the people around you." Mankind was made in God's image; to love God is to also love humanity. To truly impact the world, we must see people the way God sees them. We must love others for the same reasons that God loves them.

The human race can seem messed up at times, but there is also a potential for every person to imitate God. Jesus would not have died for us if he did not believe that we had the chance to be something magnificent. Jesus saw what God sees in the world: Even though people are in the darkness and full of sin, they are also capable of bringing light with the help of the Holy Spirit.

I have seen and heard so many inspiring examples of young men and women who are out there making a difference for God.

> A teen girl from Los Angeles, California, became president of the Christian Club at her high school, and through the small group Bible studies they hosted, she was able to baptize her close friend. The two of them later ended up studying the Bible with and helping to baptize one of their friends from elementary school.

> A girl I know in the teen ministry in Cambodia is working with an organization that helps save young girls from becoming prostitutes (prostitution by impoverished young girls is a huge problem in Cambodia).

A group of teens from Athens, Georgia, has traveled to Jamaica the past few summers to host weeklong camps for Jamaican teens. Fourteen teens have already become disciples because of the influence of these camps, and the Athens group plans to return to the island every summer. They have already expanded their program, now called The Swamp Corps, and traveled to Johannesburg, South Africa, where they recently hosted a camp for 185 campers from six African nations. Talk about worldwide impact!

There are many ways to live the way that Jesus calls us to live in Matthew 25:

- You can devote yourself to one-on-one relationships with other Christians, with the goal of helping one another to become more like Jesus.
- You can serve the poor.
- You can invite people to church or to study the Bible together.
- You can join an evangelistic Bible discussion at school.
- If there isn't one, you can start one at your school.

There's no single "right way" to impact the world. The beauty is that God gives us the freedom to develop our own vision for how to impact the world around us. God created us to do all of these great things, but we need to do it voluntarily and with our whole heart. We must serve God because we want to and not because others expect us to. When it comes to salvation, the path is narrow, but when we walk on that path, the possibilities are endless! We must share our faith with the world—*our* faith, not our parents' or teen leaders' faith.

The Dual Ministry of Jesus

Jesus stepped into a boat, crossed over and came to his own town. Some men brought to him a paralyzed man, lying on a mat. When Jesus saw their faith, he said to the man, "Take heart, son; your sins are forgiven."

At this, some of the teachers of the law said to themselves, "This fellow is blaspheming!"

Knowing their thoughts, Jesus said, "Why do you entertain evil thoughts in your hearts? Which is easier: to say, 'Your sins are forgiven,' or to say, 'Get up and walk'? But so that you may know that the Son of Man has authority on earth to forgive sins..." Then he said to the paralytic, "Get up, take your mat and go home." Then the man got up and went home. (Matthew 9:1–7)

Some people call Jesus' ministry a "dual ministry" because he cared for people's physical needs and spiritual needs. He forgave people's sins and also healed their physical diseases. He fed people literally by giving them food to eat, and he also fed their souls with the word of God. I love the way Jesus cared for the entire person.

I have worked hard to imitate this part of Jesus' example in my own life. I have learned that when I get in touch with people's physical and emotional needs, it helps me to better understand their spiritual needs. I have learned that when people see that I study the Bible with others and I also serve the poor, they know I am a Christian.

Since Jesus had a ministry, I think I should have one as well! My ministry is the group of people that God has put in my life to help. Obviously I can't heal diseases or forgive sin as Jesus did, but I can show people the gospel and care for their physical needs if they are ill. Whether it is the young men that I mentor, the people I am studying the Bible with, the people I serve who are less fortunate than I am, my own friends who need moral support, or even the people who mentor me, all of these people are part of the ministry of Drew, which is a small portion of the ministry of Jesus.

I work hard to model what I do after how Jesus ran his own ministry. I even try to get advice from people who actually run ministries so they can help me learn how to meet people's needs better. I may not be a church leader, but I can still live my life in a way that cares for the physical and spiritual needs of the people around me.

- Who do you know now that you can minister to?
- Do you have friends you can study the Bible with?
- How can you meet the needs of your friends and family?
- How can you serve people who are less fortunate than you?

World impact starts with our love for God, who loves us so much that he gave us his Son Jesus. The example of Jesus shows that the way we treat the people around us is a window into our love for God. Show your love for God by loving other people, and you will impact the world.

GET REAL

1. In what ways has growing up in the church equipped you to make an impact on other people?
2. In many ways God says in Scripture: "If you want to serve me, serve the people around you." When we love others, we are showing love for God. How does knowing this motivate you to make a difference in people's lives?
3. Jesus was focused on meeting physical and spiritual needs in people's lives. Which is more natural and easy for you to do? How can you grow in the other area?

KEEPING IT REAL
Searching for a Vision

Halfway through college, I decided to go to Cambodia for a summer to help serve the poor and to visit the church in Phnom Penh. I really had no idea how God would use me there; I just knew it was something I needed to do. I had always heard that life in America was easier compared to life in developing countries, but I had never seen it for myself. I wanted to better understand poverty and learn how to help. Little did I know that my time in Cambodia would change my future in amazing ways.

I stood there in the slums outside the city of Phnom Penh and realized that my life in the States was far better than I had ever realized. Some of the people I met in Cambodia had no power, no bathrooms and no clean water. The government had forced them out of their homes in the city to make room for more commercial buildings. There was no justice for these people, nothing they could do, no one to speak for them.

Back home in Los Angeles, I had luxuries at my fingertips that people in poor countries would never have an opportunity to have or even see for themselves.

That moment, standing in the slums, changed my whole perspective on life. I began to develop a vision for my life to serve the poor as Jesus did. I had so much in the States, and I wanted to learn how to give back.

Later that week when I was hanging out with Cesar Lopez, the leader of the church in Phnom Penh, he said, "Hey bro, there is a young guy here who has been studying the Bible. I have a study with him today, and I'd love to have you join us if you're free."

"Sure, sounds good," I said, without really thinking much about it.

I went into Brian Liu's Bible study later that afternoon expecting to share a few thoughts here and there, and that's it. But I found out that Brian was a Kingdom Kid, just like me. His parents were running one of the HOPE *worldwide* projects in the city, and he had no other Kingdom Kids to relate to in the Phnom Penh church.

I realized that Brian had a lot of struggles that were similar to those I had gone through. I ended up building a great friendship with him during my stay in Phnom Penh. I made sure I was in the rest of his studies, and I was even able to witness his baptism later that month!

God had planned for Brian and me to be friends; it was obvious. Brian needed the extra help from a fellow Kingdom Kid who understood the struggles of growing up going to church. And I needed the extra help from a fellow Kingdom Kid to realize there were teens all over the world who loved God and wanted to live their lives for Jesus. Brian was a great example to me of a young man who had a humble heart and was willing to learn even though he had grown up in the church and knew the Scriptures.

The summer of 2009 changed my life. From then on it became my dream to go back to the developing world to serve the poor and bring people to Christ. Two years later, when I graduated from college, I moved back to Cambodia to continue to learn how to meet needs and save souls. Even now as I write this book, I am working in Cambodia and ministering to people.

Spiritual Dreams and Vision

In John 14:12 Jesus says,

> "I tell you the truth, anyone who has faith in me will do what I have been doing. He will do even greater things than these, because I am going to the Father."

Kingdom Kids have unlimited potential and a very special role in advancing the gospel to this generation. Jesus told his disciples that they would do even greater things than they had already seen. Although I imagine it must have been pretty difficult for them to believe his words, this did indeed come true! With the Holy Spirit leading the way, the disciples and the apostles spread the gospel throughout the world.

Even though some of them were tortured and killed, the first-century Christians defied the Roman Empire, the most powerful empire in the whole world. In the moment it may not have seemed as though these followers of Christ were living as free people—they were imprisoned and punished for their faith—but it was only a matter of time before Christianity had taken over the entire Roman Empire.

Since then, the name of Jesus has spread across the globe. Countless numbers of people have heard the message of the gospel because the followers of Jesus Christ have chosen to fight for their spiritual vision and spread the word of God.

Jesus' words are just as true today as they were back then. He wants us to use the amazing gifts of freedom and the Holy Spirit to do amazing things in his name.

Great Possibilities

Irenaeus, an influential leader in the early church, said that "the glory of God is man fully alive." A beautiful thing about God (among many beautiful things) is that he is eternal. He always has been, always is, and always will be...and he wants us to start treating our own soul the same way. God wants us to learn from the *past*, so we can begin doing things *now* to improve the *future*. In order to be able to be "fully alive" as disciples of Christ, we must be able to recognize and live with the freedom that he died for.

Once we have let go of our fears and anxieties about what other people think about us and want for us, we will begin to think more positively and more clearly about how we want to live for God.

There is so much we can do with the blessings that he has given us as Kingdom Kids. It is crucial that we all work to develop a clear vision of how we will proceed to advance the glory of God in the world. Jobs and careers can be a great part of our lives, but they are simply what we do so that we can continue living the Christian life. God gives us money to provide for our needs and to enable us to give to others.

If you have come to the point where what you want most in life is a relationship with God, then you are ready to be as free as

God made you to be. The great part about this is that it's not the end—it is just the beginning of an extraordinary journey! The possibilities are endless. It is time for you to begin thinking about how you can most effectively work for the glory of God.

When I left Cambodia that summer to begin my junior year in college, I had no idea that two years later God would bring me back to live in this country and continue to serve those in need. I am writing this chapter from the wonderful city of Phnom Penh, where I am living and praying and working alongside amazing disciples of Jesus who encourage and inspire me.

I studied business in college, and it is so exciting to be able to use the skills I learned in school to help the poor. God has blessed me with great opportunities in the mission field to serve in hospitals and other nonprofits. There are also many teens in Cambodia who need the help of a fellow Kingdom Kid in learning how to find real freedom in their relationship with God. The mission field is truly my calling, and I can't wait to see how God uses me in the coming years.

Different Gifts for Different People

Paul tells us in 1 Corinthians 12:4-7 that God has given every disciple different gifts:

> There are different kinds of gifts, but the same Spirit. There are different kinds of service, but the same Lord. There are different kinds of working, but the same God works all of them in all men.
>
> Now to each one the manifestation of the Spirit is given for the common good.

One great thing about serving God is that he knows us better than we know ourselves, and he knows exactly where to put us so that we can be both happy and effective in our work to save the world. Without getting too technical, the Greek word that Paul used in this scripture for "gift" was *charismata*, and *charismata* is a root word for the English word "charismatic."

What are you charismatic about? What are you passionate about? What do you love doing that you are also good at? I'll bet you can find a great way to use that gift of yours to glorify God.

A friend of mine is a very talented athlete. Because of his talent, he is able to influence athletes in ways that other people can't. So what does he do? He brings a different athlete from school to church nearly every Sunday!

I know a girl who has an amazing voice, and she loves to sing. However, instead of pursuing any type of singing career, she loves to sing at church in a way that glorifies God.

Other friends have gifts of encouragement, organization, serving...I could go on about all of the talented people I know who are using their gifts to pursue whatever spiritual vision they have to serve God.

My passion for the past few years has been to help manage nonprofit organizations that serve the poor in the developing world. It is my "charisma" and my spiritual dream to live my life doing this, and God has blessed me with amazing opportunities. God can do the same thing for you. It just takes having a genuine relationship with God and a passion to serve him and the people around you. God wants to use you—and he *will*—if you begin to develop a spiritual vision for your life.

Where to Go From Here

So we come back to the same question I asked toward the beginning of this book: *What do you want?* What do you really want for your spiritual life? I hope you'll answer that question differently now that you've read this book. I hope that now you'll consider the will of God before you consider your own.

If you want to please God more than anything, using all the gifts he has given you—including your unique experiences as a Kingdom Kid—it will be amazing to see how God connects your will with his and enables you to do great things for him. As Paul put it, God can use you to do "immeasurably more than all [you] ask or imagine, according to his power that is at work within [you]" (Ephesians 3:20).

Everyone wants to be free; freedom is one of the most valuable things in life. Amazingly, freedom is attainable by anyone who wants a relationship with God, and yet only a few people in this world find true freedom. Human beings around the world struggle to find meaning in all the hardship and confusion that they face. Kingdom Kids go through this same struggle in their own unique ways.

God wants us to be like him. He wants us to love as he loves, desire what he desires, and be free as he is free. He wants this for us because he knows that this is the only way we can find true peace. He wants this for us because he loves us.

Kingdom Kids are indeed free—in fact, we enjoy far more freedom than many other people around us! God has spared us from so many of the struggles that other people are chained by from the moment they enter this world. So many of our friends are born into unhappy families that don't know how to get along, or broken families dealing with divorce; so many of our friends are exposed to things like drugs and pornography that our parents did their best to protect us from; so many of our friends bear scars from the extra "freedom" they had to experiment with hurtful things like alcohol and sex.

Freedom for Life

It is important that we appreciate the freedom and free will God has given us so that we can live a successful Christian life. I hope this book has helped you to appreciate the gift it is to be a Kingdom Kid. I hope it's helped you to see that it is a joy and a privilege, not a burden and a requirement. I hope it has helped you to understand the difference between fake freedom and real freedom. I hope it's helped you to unravel some of the complicated feelings we can have when we get too concerned about other people's expectations and forget to live for God. I hope it's helped you to differentiate between others' faith and your own faith.

The apostle Paul, referencing the Old Testament, wrote to the Corinthians saying, "I tell you, now is the time of God's favor, now is the day of salvation" (2 Corinthians 6:2). There is no better time than now to begin working on your vision for the future. There are so many needs around the world, so many people searching desperately for the type of freedom that we have found in Jesus. Will you be able to lead them there?

The powerful story of salvation will continue through the ages, and God has left plenty of room for you to contribute a verse. What will your verse be?

GET REAL

1. What are some talents God has given you that you can use to encourage others?
2. Have you ever let yourself dream about ways you can serve God when you are older? What are these dreams, and who can you talk to and get direction and help to see them come true?

3. If you are not aware of either your talents or your dreams, how can you get more in touch?

4. As you have now finished reading this book from one Kingdom Kid to another, what three perspectives or nuggets of truth have you gotten from it, and how do you see these changing you in your walk with God?

Other Resources

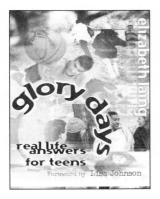

Glory Days:
Real-Life Answers for Teens
Elizabeth Laing Thompson

The teen years—the best of times or the worst of times? That is the question. Elizabeth Laing Thompson, writing fresh out of these years herself, powerfully shares her experiences—from the laugh-out-loud humorous to the painful—and the deep convictions she gained along the way.

Letters to New Disciples:
Practical Advice for Those Who
Have Decided to Follow Jesus
Thomas A. Jones

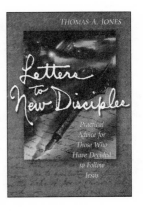

As a new disciple of Jesus, you have entered a brave new world. You have found the One who gives real life. But while your decision set off a party in heaven, it also put you right in the middle of a great struggle between darkness and light. In these 24 short letters you will find biblical direction, practical advice, and inspiring words of encouragement that will help you win the battles and enjoy the ride.

Disciples on Campus:
Challenge and Encouragement for
the 21st Century Student
Edited by Marty Fuqua and Gregg Marutzky

Though written to college students, mature high school students will benefit greatly from reading this book written mostly by people who were converted as students themselves. Input for all areas in life will help you to grow in your convictions, faith, responsibility and evangelism.